Year by Year: *The Major Events of the War*

YEAR	GENERAL	WESTERN FRONT
1914	Assassination of Archduke Ferdinand (June)	
	General war breaks out (August)	Schlieffen Plan
	Bombardment of Hartlepool, Scarborough, etc.	First battle of Marne
	Fall of Tsing Tau	First battle of Ypres
1915	Italy joins the war	Second Ypres
		Germans use poison gas
	Gallipoli	British and French breakthrough attempts
1916	Conscription in Britain	Verdun
	Lloyd George replaces Asquith as Prime Minister	Somme
1917	America joins war	Arras (Vimy Ridge)
	Italians driven back at Caporetto	
	Turks defeated	Third Ypres (Passchendaele)
		Cambrai (tanks)
1918	Royal Air Force formed	German Spring Offensive
	Armistice (November)	Second Marne
		Final Allied Offensive

EASTERN FRONT	AT SEA
Battles of Tannenberg and Masurian Lakes	*Goeben* and *Breslau* escape Heligoland Bight *Emden*'s exploits Coronel and Falklands
Breakthrough at Gorlice Russians driven back	*Lusitania* sunk
Brusilov's breakthrough	Jutland
Revolution in Russia	Greatest losses of ships to German U-boats
Russia out of war: Treaty of Brest-Litovsk	Zeebrugge

World War One

WORLD WAR ONE

Edited by P. Liddle

A collection of source material (letters, diaries, maps, paintings, posters, newspapers etc) on different aspects of the war. The booklets and pupils workbooks are available separately.

The Booklets:	*Teachers Pack:*
The Western Front	Newspapers (16 pages)
The Domestic Front	Four teaching maps
Other Fronts	1 copy of each booklet
The War at Sea and in the Air	A set of pupils workbooks
Gallipoli	Teacher's booklet
Letters to a Country Rector	
Conscientious Objection	
Commendation, Casualty and Captivity	

THE GREAT WAR

Edited by Tony Howarth

For CSE pupils the 12 Units in this series provide resource-based material on the main aspects of the war. A programme of work is built into the text of each booklet, to encourage pupils to interpret and evaluate evidence.

This Project is available on subscription from the Longman Group Resources Unit, 9–11 The Shambles, York.

Making the Modern World
WORLD WAR I

D.B. O'Callaghan

A short, highly illustrated, topic book.

WORLD WAR I

Dudley Woodget

A sketchmap history of the war.

FILMSTRIPS

THE FIRST WORLD WAR
W.F. Norton. Common Ground Filmstrips
Single frame; black and white.

WORLD WAR ONE
Edited by Peter Liddle
2 strips, double & single frame; colour.

MODERN TIMES

World War One

S. R. Gibbons

P. Morican

LONGMAN

LONGMAN GROUP LIMITED
London

*Associated companies, branches and representatives
throughout the world*

First published 1965
Twelfth impression 1980

ISBN 0 582 20421 6

*Printed in Hong Kong by
Wing King Tong Co Ltd*

Acknowledgements

We are grateful to the following for permission to reproduce
copyright material:

The Beaverbrook Archives for material from *War Memoirs*, Vol. 2
by David Lloyd George; Cassell & Co. Ltd for 'Abdul' by
C.E.W.B. from *The Anzac Book*; Cassell & Co. Ltd and
W. W. Norton & Company, Inc. for material from *The Last
Act* by Barrie Pitt; Constable & Co. Ltd for material from
Peacemaking 1919 by Sir Harold Nicolson; Hutchinson & Co.
(Publishers) Ltd for material from *Modern Spies Tell Their Stories*
edited and compiled by R. W. Rowan, and *The Fighting at
Jutland* by H. W. Fawcett and G. W. Hooper; Odhams Press
Ltd and Charles Scribner's Sons for material from *The World
Crisis* by Winston S. Churchill; Mr. Harold Owen, Chatto and
Windus Ltd and New Directions for 'The Letter' and 'The
Chances' by Wilfred Owen from *The Collected Poems of Wilfred
Owen*, © Chatto and Windus 1963, and Virtue & Co. Ltd for
material from *The Great War in Europe* by Frank R. Cana.
The English newspaper cutting on pages 108 and 109 is
reproduced by permission of the *Daily Mirror* and the panoramic
photograph on pages 112 and 113 is by permission of the
Ministry of Defence. All other photographs are by courtesy of
the Imperial War Museum, whose staff have been unfailingly
helpful, with the exception of those on pages 11, 12 and 41, the
original sources of which we have been unable to trace.

Preface

It is hoped that this book will be found suitable for general school use, both formally and informally. It is aimed at the average child of secondary school age, and the general historical narrative is interspersed with accounts of the personal experiences of some of those who took part. By this means, we hope that the human element will be accorded its rightful place of eminence among the facts and figures.

No book of this size could treat so complex a subject without many omissions, and some material has inevitably had to be sacrificed to the main aim: to present a graphic, interesting account of this most fateful of wars for the many modern young people who are at last beginning to study modern history.

For their personal recollections of the events of the war, or for other assistance, we are grateful to the following: L. Russell; W. Wheeler; G. Pearson; N. Hunt (née Bibby); F. Newall; T. Aldous; D. Hurd; A. Ashton; L. Snellgrove; C. Richards; J. Metcalfe; G. Laurie; J. Foard; P. Ager; B. Mason; the Italian and Turkish military attachés.

S. R. Gibbons
P. Morican

Contents

1   Events Leading to the Outbreak of the War

The Murders that Rocked the World 28 June 1914

Loud cheers rang through the air from the crowds who lined the gaily decorated streets of Sarajevo, capital city of the Austrian province of Bosnia. The citizens were cheering the royal visitors who were on a state visit to their town. From their open car Archduke Ferdinand, Prince of Austria, and his wife Countess Sophie smiled their approval and waved to their admirers. They were quite unaware that mingling with the happy crowds of citizens was a young Serbian named Gavrilo Princip, who, as a member of the Black Hand Secret Society, had sworn an oath to kill the royal couple.

Suddenly the royal car jerked to a halt. The driver realized that he had taken a wrong turning and slowly the vehicle began to reverse. Princip seized his chance. He stepped forward and from a distance of about six feet fired two shots before the startled police escort could do anything. Both shots proved fatal. The first bullet smashed through the car door and struck Countess Sophie, who died within a few minutes. The second bullet struck the Archduke in the neck, and within half an hour he too had died.

The angry crowd surged round the struggling Princip. It took several minutes to overpower him and drag him away to gaol and trial.

The world was horrified at the dreadful deed. When the Austrians heard of the murder of their prince and his wife they were very angry and accused the Government of Serbia of deliberately planning the murders. They prepared their troops for a war of revenge.

The Great Powers of Europe all took sides. Within a few weeks the deaths of those two people had led to a war which eventually cost ten million lives.

Why was it that the Great Powers were so ready to enter

such a gigantic and costly struggle—possibly the worst war the world has ever seen? Why was there so much suspicion and enmity in the Europe of 1914?

One of the main reasons was the rise of a new and powerful state: Germany.

A New Neighbour for France and Russia: The German Empire

The two sketch maps will show you how Germany developed into a large and powerful state in Europe.

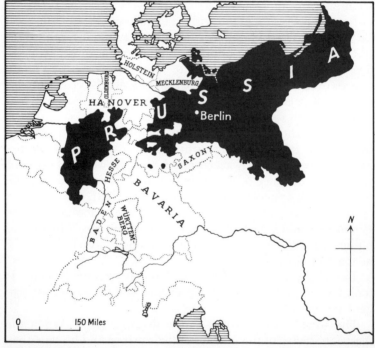

Germany in 1848
Before Germany was unified this is what she looked like on a map—lots of small states, all with their own governments and all competing with one another. (Think what would happen if all the counties of England had their own governments and competed with one another!)

In the new Germany there was a great respect for the soldier and it was considered an honour to fight for the state. Both Russia and France feared the new German Army, for as you

2

can see from the map on this page both lay on the German borders and might be invaded in case of war.

But the new Germany was not content with a large army alone. Her rulers wanted a large navy as well. 'Our future lies on the water,' said the Emperor William (the Kaiser), and on another occasion: 'I must first get for myself a fleet.' So the Germans began to build a large navy.

The British were alarmed by this large German fleet. Was it meant to be used against Britain? After all, the German Army

Germany United, 1871
Notice the difference. The man who was chiefly responsible for the unification of Germany was Bismarck. He made Germany strong and showed her strength by defeating both Austria and France in short, bitter wars (1866 and 1870). He managed to make friends again with Austria, but France thirsted for revenge. . . .

was already the most powerful in Europe, and it did seem as though the Germans were determined to become stronger than any other country. And so, a 'naval race' arose between the

3

The German Battle-Cruiser *Goeben*, launched in 1912

two countries, with both Britain and Germany trying to build up their fleets as fast as possible.

The other great European Powers also found themselves in competition with the new Germany. Germany wanted a greater share of the world's trade. She wanted colonies like those of Britain and France. Her statesmen grew bolder and began to use threats to gain their way. The other nations became anxious and fearful.

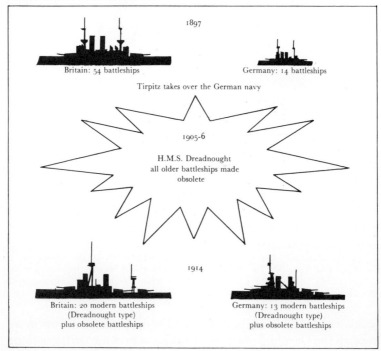

1897

Britain: 54 battleships   Germany: 14 battleships

Tirpitz takes over the German navy

1905-6

H.M.S. Dreadnought
all older battleships made
obsolete

1914

Britain: 20 modern battleships   Germany: 13 modern battleships
(Dreadnought type)   (Dreadnought type)
plus obsolete battleships   plus obsolete battleships

The Growth of the Two Navies

The Great Powers began to form alliances among themselves because they were each afraid to stand alone. By 1914 Europe was divided into two armed camps:

The Triple Alliance	*The Triple Entente*
Germany, Austria, Italy	Russia, France, Britain

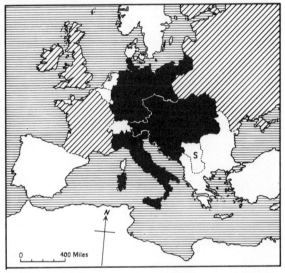

The Armed Groups in Europe. The Entente powers are lined; the Central powers are in black. Serbia is marked with an 'S'

When the unfortunate Franz Ferdinand was murdered at Sarajevo the European Powers, already armed to the teeth, set their soldiers on the march. Germany supported the Austrians in their attack on Serbia. France and Russia opposed them. The Italians, for the time being, decided to remain neutral.

Why did Britain enter the war? Along with the other powers she had signed a treaty seventy-five years earlier, promising never to attack the little state of Belgium, and to oppose any who did so. Within eight weeks of the Sarajevo murders German soldiers were pouring into Belgium, on their way to invade France. What would Britain do? Forget the treaty she had signed, and let the Germans have their way? Or keep her word?

The Germans should not have been surprised to find Britain

5

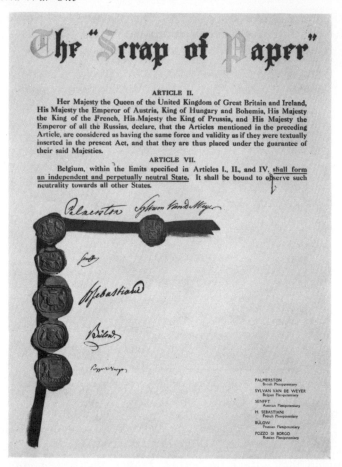

The Treaty of London, 1839, promising support for a neutral Belgium

so interested in Belgium and the treaty of 1839. Over the centuries a great deal of British trade had depended on this part of Europe: particularly on the ports of Flanders. They had spelt prosperity to the English wool trade since the time of Henry VIII and earlier. They were a gateway to Europe for British goods. But in enemy hands they could spell disaster, for the whole Flanders area made a natural springboard for an invasion of Britain. From the British point of view it was essential that the Belgians, like their Dutch neighbours, should remain independent of the great continental Powers. Most Britons also felt that it was essential that solemnly made treaties should be observed. Indeed, many Germans felt the same way, and were very disturbed when their armies crossed the border on their way to France. But by that time things had gone too far, and the tragedy could not be halted.

A Memorable Interview

It was Tuesday evening, 4 August 1914. The Great Powers of Europe, with the exception of Britain, were at war, their huge armies already on the march. The Germans hoped that the British would stay out of the conflict; the French that their new-found friendship with Britain would bring her into the war as an ally.

In Berlin Sir Edward Goschen, the British Ambassador, was on his way to see the German Chancellor. The message he carried made his visit the most urgent and important of his life. That very day German troops had invaded Belgium, and Sir Edward's message from London made it quite clear that unless the invasion were halted Britain would enter the war against Germany.

Sir Edward found the Imperial Chancellor, Herr Bethmann-Hollweg, in a bad temper. Like most Germans, he had counted on Britain's remaining outside any European conflict. The atmosphere became electric as Sir Edward delivered his message. This mentioned the 1839 Treaty of London, by which both Britain and Germany had guaranteed the neutrality of Belgium. The British note asked for a satisfactory answer by midnight, failing which war would follow. Both men knew that the German plans had gone too far to be halted, and that the British attitude therefore made war inevitable. Bethmann-Hollweg became excited and indignant. How could Britain strike such a blow at a kindred nation? She was entering the war over a single word, neutrality, merely for a 'scrap of paper'. She would be responsible for all the horrors that would follow.

Sir Edward listened quietly until the angry words were over. Even then he said very little, merely remarking that the British Government felt that its solemn promise of 1839 must be kept. He left to make final preparations for leaving Berlin.

During the rest of the evening a mob of angry Germans gathered at the British Embassy, throwing stones and shouting 'Traitors!'. The minutes ticked away to midnight. The 'satisfactory reply' did not arrive, and the two nations were at war. Germany had indeed regarded the seventy-five-year-old treaty as a mere 'scrap of paper', whereas Britain had honoured it to the letter. It was to cost both nations dearly.

We should be careful not to lay all the blame for the war on Germany. Although the Germans were far too ready to use their great military strength, and their invasion of Belgium was a callous disregard for a weaker people who happened to stand in their way, the other European nations had been too suspicious and unwilling to accept the new state as an equal partner. Jealousy and fear had played their parts and made a difficult situation dangerous and explosive.

The German Soldier of 1914

2 The Land War I: In France

The Schlieffen Plan for a Knock-out Blow against France

As soon as the war started the Germans put into action their long-prepared Schlieffen Plan.

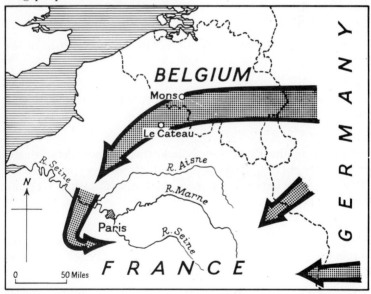

The German Plan of 1914, named after Count von Schlieffen

By this plan their troops would pour through Belgium (whose unfortunate people wished only to live in peace), race across northern France, where there were few modern forts, and first by-pass, then capture, Paris. The French armies would then be caught in a huge encircling movement, and France would be beaten. German troops could then be taken to the east to meet the expected attack of the large Russian

9

armies. With France crushed it was hoped that Britain, having only a small army, would make peace. But the Plan went wrong:

1   The Belgians fought bravely and slowed down the advance of the German Army.

2   The French armies, though retreating, were not beaten or encircled, and were able to strike back.

3   The British sent their troops across to France with amazing speed, and they succeeded in stemming the German advance first at Mons, then at Le Cateau.

DIARY OF THE VITAL WEEKS

4 August 1914
The Plan begins. German troops invade Belgium.

5–14 August
Belgian forts resist strongly, but fall to the heavy guns of the Germans.

20 August
The Plan goes on. German forces capture Brussels, the Belgian capital.

29 August
A Change in the Plan. Von Kluck, the German general, decides not to encircle Paris as planned. He swerves eastwards to close the gap between his own and neighbouring German forces.

5 September
The Plan is nearest to success. The German armies are now across the River Marne and very near Paris. French troops are rushed to the front in Paris taxis.

6 September
The Plan in danger. Joffre, the French commander, launches his big counter-attack. The battle of the Marne rages for the following week. . . .

13 September
The Plan fails. The Germans lose the battles on the Marne and retreat to the river Aisne.

By the end of September both sides had begun to dig

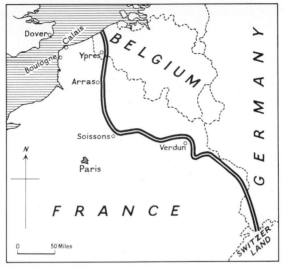

The Line of the Trenches, early 1915

trenches. These eventually stretched in an unbroken line across northern France, from Switzerland to the sea.

How the French saw it. A cartoon postcard showing the Belgian fortress town of Liège resisting the invaders (and giving a good account of itself!)

After the failure of their Schlieffen Plan the Germans made a final desperate effort to snatch the speedy victory they needed. Using their forces in Belgium, they struck hard towards the vital Channel ports: Calais and Boulogne. The British forces, moved up from the Marne area, met them before the Belgian town of Ypres. The fighting was murderous and bitter. Nearer the sea, the Belgians flooded part of the land to stop the advance. After six weeks' furious fighting Ypres was still in Allied hands and the ports were safe. But British casualties numbered about fifty thousand men who could ill be spared; and it is estimated that the French lost equally heavily. They had taken an even heavier toll of the German attackers.

La Misérable petite Armée du Général French

As the French saw it. A cartoon postcard showing the British Expeditionary Force in Action

The Belgian 'Atrocities'

As the German armies poured into Belgium during the hot August of 1914 ugly stories about their behaviour began to spread. Ordinary civilians were said to have been brutally ill-treated and sometimes killed, for no apparent reason. Women and children had been shot. The newspapers of France, Britain and America took up the reports, and many Belgian refugees added their own accounts. Public opinion all over the world turned against the Germans as stories of 'German frightfulness' grew.

From the German side there were many protests that the reports were invented or exaggerated. Most of them were. German commanders in Belgium were faced with the problem of how to deal with the *franc-tireurs*, Belgian civilians who armed themselves and fired on the grey-uniformed soldiers as they passed along the dusty roads and through the villages. As always in war, the innocent suffered with the guilty. This was particularly true when the Germans took hostages from the villages: groups of people whose lives were to be forfeited if there were any attacks on soldiers in the district.

The full truth about the Belgian atrocities is still not known; war produces such reports on both sides. But even if true only in part the reports caused a great upsurge of feeling against the Germans throughout the world.

The Trench Warfare of the Western Front

In northern France the two sides faced one another from their trenches. This type of warfare was to continue for the next three and a half years, with the network of trenches gradually becoming more and more complicated, and the defences more and more formidable. Sometimes there would be furious and bitter fighting across the 'No Man's Land' between the two lines, and perhaps one side would gain a little ground.

Life in the trenches. The weather too could be an enemy. A flooded dugout in a front-line trench in Flanders

Life in the trenches. A German officer firing a Maxim gun from a front-line trench in the Marne area

Life in the trenches. A Lewis gun post in a forward area, manned by Seaforth Highlanders, 1917

Life in the trenches. A ration party with food containers, Arras, 1917

Death in the trenches. German soldiers lie dead in their trench: above them a British tank, hit by gunfire. A picture from the Cambrai battle of 1917, when the tanks did so well

15

Sometimes there would be but little activity save for patrols of a few men who would be sent out from their positions to keep an eye on the enemy, or perhaps to make a brief raid.

During this war machine-guns were used in large numbers, and caused frightful casualties on either side. The gun positions were often protected by sandbags or banks of earth, as well as by tangled masses of barbed wire; and the Germans especially built many concrete emplacements. Each post could not only defend itself but would be supported by the 'cross-fire' of the positions on each side, so that any attacks would be met by a tremendous hail of bullets.

The front-line trench would usually be deep enough for men to walk along without showing themselves to the enemy. In order to man the trench and see over the parapet it was necessary to stand slightly higher, on the firing step. Walking along the trench one would pass the entrances to the dugouts, sometimes hardly more than a depression in the wall, but sometimes stoutly made and proof against anything but a direct hit by a shell. The trenches changed direction frequently: a raiding group must not be able to sweep the whole position with their weapons. The British built movable barriers of stakes and barbed wire which were kept in the recesses made for them, or swung aside on hinges, till they should be needed. Then they could be moved to form an obstacle to any German troops which might manage to overrun the first position.

Night attacks would be lit by 'star-shells' which burst low in the sky to light up all around with a ghastly silver glare. Often the attack would follow a bombardment of the enemy positions by the guns, which were placed at varying distances behind the trenches. The soldiers would hear the shells whine past overhead, to burst on or near the enemy positions, scattering shrapnel and metal fragments in all directions.

Shells which exploded in the ground made craters which were often large enough to become death-traps when full of water, in the winter. At these times there were places where it was impossible to move about without 'duck-boards', to prevent sinking into the mud.

To be caught in an artillery bombardment could be a shattering experience, resulting for many in death or mutilation. Guns and howitzers could be massed together against a short

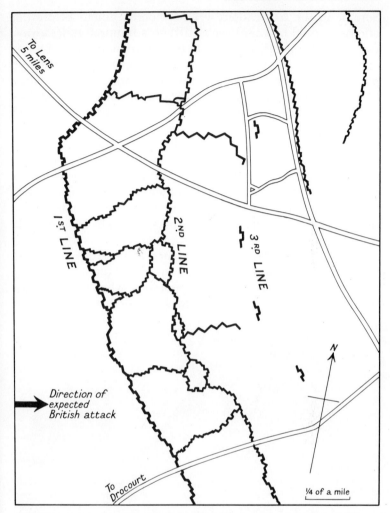

To Lens
5 miles

1ST LINE

2ND LINE

3RD LINE

N

Direction of
expected
British attack

To
Drocourt

¼ of a mile

Typical arrangement of trenches. Part of the Hindenburg Line. The third line of trench positions is not completed

stretch of front in such force that their combined effect was far beyond anything imagined before 1914. Around the French fortress-town of Verdun, for example, the crash and roar of the thousands of guns involved in the great struggle of 1916 scarcely ceased, and could be heard fifty miles away quite plainly. When the wind was right the British gunfire on the

17

Somme in the tremendous week of bombardment before the offensive could be heard even in Kent, a hundred miles away. It is difficult to realize what this meant to the troops. Modern high-explosive shells proved of such horrifying destructive power that it is no wonder the minds of some gave way. They had to face not only the prospect of death or terrible injuries for themselves, but often to see at close quarters the pitiful remains of others, torn, mangled and even stained to a ghastly yellow by the new explosive, lyddite. Thousands of men suffered from 'shell-shock', and had to be brought out of the line for convalescence and treatment. Many of these developed a stammer, or other difficulties with their speech; some the gun-fire left trembling uncontrollably in every limb, unable to do the simplest task; and some were utterly dazed by their terrible experiences.

Worse horrors still awaited the men in the front lines. The Germans used poison gas in April 1915, choking and blinding the British, Indian and French soldiers who, without gas-masks, opposed them: and the British invented the tank, which

A 15-in. howitzer in action during the Ypres fighting of 1917

created a panic among the German infantry when it was first
used in 1916.

To be 'up the line' during the great battles was indeed to
live side by side with death in a multitude of awful forms.
After the war the survivors were to find themselves bound together by experiences which it was impossible to describe ade-
quately to those who had not been there.

The Letter: WILFRED OWEN

With B.E.F. June 10. Dear Wife,
(O blast this pencil. 'Ere, Bill, lend's a knife.)
I'm in the pink at present, dear.
I think the war will end this year.
We don't see much of them square-'eaded 'Uns.
We're out of harm's way, not bad fed.
I'm longing for a taste of your old buns.
(Say, Jimmie, spare's a bite of bread.)
There don't seem much to say just now.
(Yer what? Then don't, yer ruddy cow!
And give us back me cigarette!)
I'll soon be 'ome. You mustn't fret.
My feet's improvin', as I told you of.
We're out in rest now. Never fear.
(VRACH! By crumbs, but that was near.)
Mother might spare you half a sov.
Kiss Nell and Bert. When me and you—
(Eh? What the 'ell! Stand to? Stand to?
Jim, give's a hand with pack on, lad.
Guh! Christ! I'm hit. Take 'old. Aye, bad.
No, damn your iodine. Jim? 'Ere!
Write my old girl, Jim, there's a dear.)

The Search for the Breakthrough

The generals of both sides hoped to break the deadlock of
trench warfare. They thought that if only they could smash
through the enemy lines into the unfortified country beyond
the war would again become a fast-moving affair, with the
cavalry regiments playing a full part. Their efforts to make the
breakthrough brought about the bitterest and worst battles in
human history, and cost literally millions of lives.

We may list the 'breakthrough attempts' of 1915 like this:

PLACE	ATTACKERS	DATE	RESULT
Champagne, 20 miles East of Rheims	French	Jan.-March	Small gain in ground (up to 5 miles), no breakthrough.
Neuve Chapelle	British	March	Less than a mile gained, no breakthrough.
Ypres	German	April	Up to four miles of ground gained near Ypres, but no breakthrough.
Vimy	French	May-June	About two miles gained, no breakthrough.
Aubers Ridge and Festubert	British	May	Less gains than previously (about ½ mile). No breakthrough.
Champagne	French	September	Gains less than two miles, no breakthrough.
Vimy	French	September	A little high ground gained, no breakthrough.
Loos	British	September	Small area gained, but no breakthrough.

The Search for the Breakthrough. The Offensives of 1915 and 1916

You will see that most of these great attacks were carried out by the Allies. The Germans had decided to remain on the defensive in the West, keeping their main efforts for the Russian Front. The lesson of 1915 was that the defence was always stronger than the attack. Even so both sides planned yet more tremendous efforts for the following year.

THE BATTLE OF VERDUN, 1916

Here the Germans hoped to destroy the French armies by attacking a short strip of the front in great force. The French would have to rush in every man available, and then the Germans would 'bleed France to death', and bring her to defeat. The battle raged for over six months, amid scenes of unparalleled horror which have left their marks on the minds of Frenchmen to this day. The attackers closed in on their objective, but the French were determined Verdun should not fall. Wave after wave of French infantrymen fell in counter-attack after counter-attack over the wilderness of mud which once had been the pleasant countryside near the river Meuse. The ground itself was poisoned by gas-shells and pitted with innumerable craters; in the warmer weather of the summer months the stench of rotting corpses was added to that of the fetid, stagnant pools. But the French did not collapse. 'They shall not pass!'* said General Pétain, thrilling France with his determination. And Verdun was indeed held by his weary, battered troops. By the autumn the German attacks had petered out, for the British had started their long-awaited offensive farther north.

BRITAIN'S NEW ARMIES

Britain's small peace-time army had grown enormously. Lord Kitchener had appealed for volunteers, and in a wave of patriotism which swept the whole country they had come forward in hundreds of thousands.

In 1916 these 'New Armies', sometimes called the 'Kitchener Armies', had taken over a section of the line ready for a great offensive in the valley of the river Somme. The bitter fighting lasted about four months, and the casualties mounted daily till over half a million men had fallen. The Germans lost

* *Ils ne passeront pas!*

The Kitchener Poster. Lord Kitchener's face was probably the best-known in Britain in the first two years of the war. The Government was overwhelmed with volunteers, and training camps were set up throughout the British Isles.

perhaps slightly fewer. A few miles of shell-devastated land were gained, but no breakthrough resulted. However, the German High Command realized the unpleasant truth that

WHAT BURNS SAID - 1782
HOLDS GOOD IN 1915

O! why the deuce should I repine,
And be an ill foreboder?
I'm twenty three, and five feet nine,
I'll go and be a sodger.

TAKE HIS TIP

The poetry of Burns is used in this poster, perhaps meant to appeal especially to Scotsmen.

Britain had become a first-class military power on the land as well as on the sea. More and more the war was becoming a struggle to the death between the British Empire and Imperial Germany.

23

The price of the offensive: a war cemetery. This particular one contains the graves of over 5,000 German soldiers. French and British cemeteries were just as extensive

The Big Push on the Somme

For a week the gunfire had never ceased. In their deep dugout, well lined with concrete and fitted with bunks for sleeping, a group of soldiers of a German Grenadier Regiment listened to the repeated crash of the explosions as the British shells fell in a constant rain on their trench positions up above. They were thankful it was not their turn to be out on watch, for the casualties among those who had to leave the deep shelters were very high. They were running short of food and water, and no mail had been delivered since the beginning of the bombardment. The hail of high explosive and shrapnel had cut down the movement of supplies till it had almost ceased.

How long could it go on? They all knew that a big attack would come as soon as the barrage lifted from the front line and the shells started to fall further behind them. The British Commander, Haig, had been building up his forces for months, and the 'Tommies' in the British trenches would be waiting for the order that would send them across No Man's Land. Gaps had already been cut in the British wire ready for the attacking infantry to pass through.

The noise increased, with the 'crump' of the exploding shells hardly stopping for a second. Suddenly the whole dugout vibrated with the tremendous force of a huge explosion.

Almost immediately there followed a second and a third, even closer, bringing the tin mugs clattering from their places on the wall. One of the last bottles of beer teetered over on the table, rolled to the edge and smashed itself on the floor. One of the men uttered an oath. The electric light flickered and went out. With trembling hands the corporal lit the hurricane lamp, and in the dim light the men stared round through the swirling dust. A huge crack had appeared in the concrete, running right across the ceiling and down one wall. A rat scuttled across the floor in terror. The thunder of explosions continued, some still very near, others farther away. The soldiers looked at one another, white-faced and fearful. The constant strain of the heavy bombardment had made them nervous and tense.

The young officer left for a moment to inspect the stairs up to the trenches, thirty feet above. For the second time in three days they were blocked with piles of earth and rubble. Within a few moments men were hard at work clearing them, for if the attack came and reached their lines while they were still underground they would be trapped and helpless. The officer looked at his watch. It was half-past-seven in the morning. The date was 1 July 1916, and grimly the young man reflected that the new month was starting well.

A 9·2-in. gun on a railway mounting. It is adding a contribution to the bombardment of 1 July 1916

All at once he was aware that the noise seemed farther away. The shells were falling further back, on the German rear positions and their second and third lines of trenches. The attack! He shouted his orders, and the men stumbled out of the dugout and up the steps, over the piles of rubbish and the shattered sandbags which the working party had not had time to clear. Most of the men carried a piece of heavy equipment as well as a rifle. Coughing and spluttering from the acrid fumes of cordite and the thick, floating dust, they emerged into the sunshine of a beautiful summer morning.

Half dazed as they were from the bombardment, they were shocked still more by the scene of utter confusion which met their eyes. The line of trenches had gone; the parapet of sandbags had disappeared. Everywhere were shell craters, loose earth and piles of rubble. The whole landscape seemed to have changed. Of the men on lookout duty there was no sign.

Farther up the line the men from the next dugout were already setting up their machine-guns on the lips of the craters, with the ammunition boxes stacked nearby. The officer took a cautious look towards the British trenches. A screen of smoke was rolling across No Man's Land, but the slight breeze was thinning it rapidly and he could see moving figures: hundreds of men, advancing from their positions towards the German line. His field glasses showed him that most of them were heavily laden with equipment, and that more and more were coming out of the British trenches to swell the numbers. The nearest were still three or four hundred yards away, but they were closing the gap steadily. The big push was on.

He glanced left and right. In the ragged craters where the German trenches had been lay the men under his command. The heavy machine-guns were already set up, their crews awaiting the order to begin firing. Away on the left, where the line stretched down to the river Somme, he could hear the shouts of the officers as the last stragglers were urged into position. If the British thought that their shelling had left the German line defenceless they were in for a surprise.

British losses on 1 July 1916 were over 57,000, of whom nearly 20,000 were killed or died of wounds.

The Chances : WILFRED OWEN

I mind as 'ow the night afore that show
Us five got talkin',—we was in the know.
'Over the top to-morrer; boys, we're for it.
First wave we are, first ruddy wave; that's tore it!'
'Ah well', says Jimmie,—an' 'e's seen some scrappin'—
'There ain't no more nor five things as can 'appen:
Ye get knocked out: else wounded—bad or cushy:
Scuppered: or nowt except yer feelin' mushy.

One of us got the knockout, blown to chops.
T'other was 'urt, like, losin' both 'is props.
An' one, to use the word of 'ypocrites,
'Ad the misfortoon to be took be Fritz.
Now me, I wasn't scratched, praise God Amighty,
(Though next time please I'll thank 'im for a blighty).
But poor young Jim, 'e's livin' an' 'e's not:
'E reckoned 'e'd five chances, an' 'e 'ad;
'E's wounded, killed, and pris'ner, all the lot,
The bloody lot all rolled in one. Jim's mad.

The Somme battles continued until late in the year, with
the Kitchener armies slowly advancing despite their heavy
losses. The Germans fought bitterly for every yard of ground,
and when they were forced to give up a position usually left it
unusable, or strewn with deadly booby traps to catch the unwary. Eventually the Germans retired to strong positions
which they had prepared a few miles to the rear of their line,
and the British troops advanced cautiously into the area they
had left. They found it a complete wilderness, with every
building reduced to rubble, every well poisoned, every bridge
destroyed, every road blocked and most of the trees cut down.

Undoubtedly the Somme battles included some fine victories. In one night attack nearly four miles of the German
second line of trenches were captured, and without the dreadful toll of dead which seemed inevitable in daylight. In September the best-kept secret of the war was revealed (some say
prematurely) as thirty-six tanks moved forward and helped to
gain a striking local success. November saw a huge charge of
explosives detonated under the German lines, after which the

troops pushed forward to take the fortified villages of Beaumont-Hamel and Beaucourt. Both places were completely in ruins above ground, but every cellar was a strong point and their German defenders had stocked them with ammunition, food, furniture and even electric lighting. With the occupation of these places the Somme fighting was over, for the time being.

September 1916. Troops moving to the attack. A German shell bursts near. It would be one of many

Waiting for the attack. German sentries in an advanced post. This picture was taken near the River Aisne

3 The War at Sea I

First Encounters

As soon as the war began, the British Navy in the oceans of the world imposed a virtually absolute blockade on all German commerce, and sought to destroy those ships of the German Navy which were known to be at large. The Admiralty in London was particularly worried about the battle-cruiser *Goeben*, in the Mediterranean, and about the German China Squadron, in the Pacific. Both were capable of causing great damage, and we shall in fact read of them later. Meantime, the seas were quickly cleared of all German shipping. Although a few daring captains tried to make a rapid dash for home most German vessels fled for neutral ports. The enormous sea-borne trade of the German Empire was eliminated with scarcely a blow, by the mere presence of the British squadrons. German colonies found themselves suddenly cut off from home. German factories were instantly deprived of any supplies which needed to be imported by boat. Only in the sheltered and protected Baltic did German ships still ply, though even here British submarines based on Russian ports were to create havoc as the war went on.

It is impossible to exaggerate the importance of this. Had it been the other way round, with the German fleets supreme and the Royal Navy confined to its ports the defeat of the Entente would have been speedy and certain. As it was, the grip of the blockade was relentless and fatal to Germany. Year by year its effect became more marked, till by the winter of 1917 it had become a stranglehold under which the German population suffered terribly and the German war effort was curtailed and crippled in a thousand ways.

However, all this still lay in the future during those first days after the declaration of war. The world waited with bated breath for the clash of the two navies which seemed imminent. On paper the British were the stronger, but in 1914 both sides were anxious and uncertain about the effect of two new weapons: mines and torpedoes. At the very outbreak of war the

Germans were believed to be sowing loose mines in the North Sea, intending that they should drift with the currents till a victim should come along. Moored mines were used to protect harbours, and were sown in shipping lanes expected to be used by the enemy.

The British made every preparation to meet the German fleet, should it emerge from its ports. From the Scottish bases of Scapa Flow and Rosyth the Grand Fleet operated, strong enough to overwhelm the enemy. Lighter forces kept a permanent watch in case the German ships should come out. Cruiser and destroyer flotillas based at Harwich and Dover maintained patrols in the North Sea and the Channel, always on the lookout for surface vessels and U-boats. Submarines lay quietly close in to the German coast, watching for the signs which would mean that the powerful enemy fleet was at last putting to sea.

The British had one great advantage. In the early days of the war the German cruiser *Magdeburg* had been sunk by Russian ships. A corpse was dragged from the icy waters of the Baltic. It was that of a German officer, and in his arms was firmly clasped the *Magdeburg*'s code book. The value of the find was recognized and it was sent to London. Throughout the rest of the war many of the German wireless messages could be deciphered by the Admiralty.

The first sea-battle of the war was fought barely three weeks after the Germans had begun their march through Belgium. This was in the Heligoland Bight, behind the protective German minefield. First a small number of destroyers was sent in to engage the German patrols, consisting of cruisers and destroyers. The enemy was taken completely by surprise on seeing that the British ships had penetrated the minefield. When, however, they observed that there were only a few destroyers they immediately gave chase. This was what the British wanted: for lurking further west was Admiral Beatty with the battle-cruisers. The destroyers headed straight for him, leading the pursuing Germans into the trap. It was well sprung . . . the Germans losing three cruisers in the engagement which followed: the *Köln*, the *Mainz* and the *Ariadne*, as well as a destroyer. Total British casualties on this daring expedition numbered only seventy men, compared with over a thousand

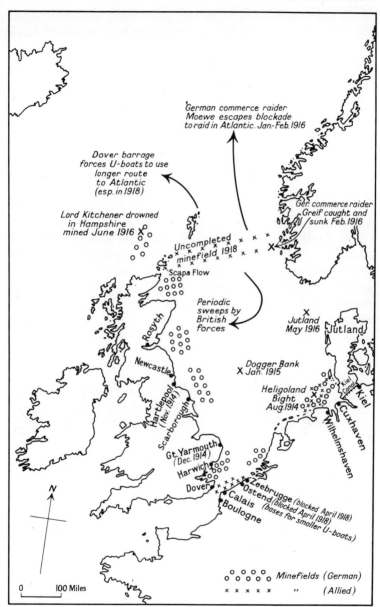

German commerce raider
Moewe escapes blockade
to raid in Atlantic. Jan.-Feb. 1916

Dover barrage
forces U-boats to use
longer route
to Atlantic
(esp. in 1918)

Ger. commerce raider
Greif caught and
sunk Feb. 1916

Lord Kitchener drowned
in Hampshire
mined June 1916 X

Uncompleted
minefield 1918

Scapa Flow

Periodic
sweeps by
British
forces

Rosyth

X
Jutland
May 1916 Jutland

Newcastle

Dogger Bank
X Jan. 1915

Heligoland
Bight
Aug. 1914

Kiel Canal

Kiel

Hartlepool
(Nov. 1914)
Scarborough

Cuxhaven

Wilhelmshaven

Gt. Yarmouth
(Dec. 1914)
Harwich

Dover

Zeebrugge (blocked April 1918)
Ostend (blocked April 1918)
(bases for smaller U-boats)

Calais
Boulogne

N

Minefields (German)
            ,,   (Allied)

0   100 Miles

The War in the North Sea

31

on the German side. In Germany great concern was felt when it was realized that the British Navy had been so successful so near the coast of Germany itself.

After this incident the Germans were more inclined to stay in their bases, but as autumn drew into winter they decided to take advantage of the long hours of darkness to sail across the North Sea, bombard coastal cities, and then return quickly. The idea was that they would terrorize the British population on the east coast, who would then insist that the Royal Navy should patrol the area in sufficient strength to protect them. This would be to the German advantage because it would mean that the British naval force would be widely strung out and would have difficulty in mustering in the event of a large-scale German attack.

The German plan was put into operation in November and December 1914, when their battle-cruisers bombarded Yarmouth, Scarborough and Hartlepool, where many people, including women and small children, were killed. After the shelling the German ships retreated to their home ports, aided by bad weather.

THIS TABLET MARKS THE PLACE
WHERE THE FIRST SHELL FROM THE
LEADING GERMAN BATTLE CRUISER
STRUCK AT 8-10 A.M. ON THE
16TH OF DECEMBER 1914
AND ALSO RECORDS THE PLACE
WHERE (DURING THE BOMBARDMENT)
THE FIRST SOLDIER WAS KILLED ON
BRITISH SOIL BY ENEMY ACTION IN
THE GREAT WAR 1914–1918.
PRESENTED BY JOHN SANDERSON ESQ
A NATIVE OF HARTLEPOOL

Inscription on Plaque at the Heugh Battery, Hartlepool

Public indignation in Britain was naturally very high, but soon came better news. In January 1915 Sir David Beatty surprised a powerful enemy force of battle-cruisers, cruisers and destroyers off Dogger Bank. They turned and fled for home, hotly pursued. For the first time in the war the most up-to-date ships of the most powerful type were in action against one another. Soon the German battle cruiser *Blücher* was in flames, and the *Seydlitz* was crippled by a salvo from the tremendous 13½-in. guns of Sir David's flagship, the *Lion*. At this crucial stage of the battle the *Lion* was hit and lost speed. Beatty signalled the rest of the squadron to continue the chase, but the

British recruiting poster, using the German bombardment of Scarborough as a spur to urge men to join up. The armies were still composed entirely of volunteers in 1915

33

message was misunderstood and the rest of the German heavy ships escaped. The *Blücher* sank, fighting bravely to the end; the *Lion* was brought home to Rosyth with an escort which included sixty destroyers, constantly circling the listing ship. Sir David Beatty's reputation, already great from his victory in the Heligoland Bight, gained a further boost.

We must not think, because the German forces fled for home, that they were cowardly. Outgunned and outnumbered, any other course would almost certainly have brought disaster.

The Most Important Ships of the War: 1 The German 'Goeben'

On the outbreak of war the German ships *Goeben* and *Breslau* were in the Mediterranean. They were expected to try to break out into the Atlantic, after first attacking the troop transports which would be ferrying French soldiers back to France from north Africa. British warships had been warned that war was about to be declared and had done their best to keep the two German vessels within striking range. But although the British fully realized the damage the *Goeben* could do in action, they had no idea at all of the tremendous part she was to play in the war. She brought Germany a new ally, Turkey, and spread the struggle throughout the whole of the Middle East.

During the few hours up to midnight the British battle-cruisers tried desperately to remain close to their powerful enemy. But the *Goeben* was new and fast, and gradually the gap widened. On both sides the captains knew the war would start at midnight, but no-one dare fire a shot till then. Those few hours made all the difference, and the *Goeben* escaped.

The British knew where she had gone, however: to the Italian port of Messina, on the island of Sicily. As Italy was still neutral the Germans would have to leave the port within twenty-four hours, and the Italians refused them the coal they needed. The battle-cruisers waited for the *Goeben* to come out, blocking the route to the Atlantic, determined that those huge guns should not have the chance to destroy British merchant ships.

On the *Goeben*, however, merchant ships were scarcely within the thoughts of Admiral Souchon. He planned to sail for Turkey, with the quite deliberate intention of forcing her into the war on the German side. He had ordered some German steamers to meet him in Messina, and during his twenty-four hours there the crew were refuelling rapidly from these vessels, whose decks were torn open and rails removed so that the precious coal could be transferred.

Souchon left the Straits of Messina in the opposite direction to that expected by the British, and so escaped their main squadron. He was, however, sighted by one cruiser stationed at the southern end of the Straits: H.M.S. *Gloucester*. A desperate chase began. The *Goeben* tried to shake off her pursuer by using all her speed, but still the British cruiser kept her in sight as they raced eastwards. Captain Kelly of the *Gloucester* could not come too close, for his ship was no match for the mighty *Goeben*. But he reported what was happening by wireless, and the British battle-cruisers joined the chase, though far behind. Another British squadron which could have intercepted the two German ships did not do so because its commander feared that his four cruisers would be sunk one by one before being able to get within range themselves.

Admiral Souchon's great problem was coal. Without more he could not reach Constantinople. He had, therefore, ordered a certain German coalship which was in the Mediterranean to disguise herself and meet him near the Greek coast. He would need a whole day to take on the fuel, so first he must shake off the *Gloucester*. He ordered the *Breslau* to slow down and to pretend to lay mines in the path of the British ship. As soon as this happened Kelly attacked the *Breslau*, and Souchon was forced to turn the *Goeben* to her aid. Kelly immediately dropped back out of range, though still in sight. The two German ships pressed on again. It seemed as though they would never shake off the British cruiser.

But now fate took a hand. Not realizing the two enemy vessels were heading for Constantinople the British thought it would be sufficient for the moment to 'bottle up' the *Goeben* and *Breslau* among the Greek islands. They could be dealt with later when the battle-cruisers had had time to arrive. And so Captain Kelly was ordered to give up the chase to avoid the risk that *Goeben* would turn and sink him. Admiral Souchon, who had no coal to spare for such manoeuvres, breathed a sigh of relief and headed north to meet the collier. *Goeben* and *Breslau* spent a whole day refuelling by a quiet little Greek island with lookouts posted on the highest ground lest the British should appear. But they had plenty of time, and went on their way to Constantinople.

Constantinople is approachable only through the narrow straits called the Dardanelles. From the land on either side, guns look down. Would the Turks allow the German ships to pass? If not, Souchon was determined to force his way through if he could. He waited anxiously for the Turks to reply to his signal, asking for a pilot. Eventually a Turkish destroyer came out to him, signalled 'Follow me', and led *Goeben* and *Breslau* through the straits toward the Turkish capital.

Once there, Souchon's guns dominated the whole city and well the Turkish Government knew it. It was only a matter of time before Turkey threw in her lot with the Germans. After all, the Germans were already fighting their hated enemies, the Russians. Officially, the Turks 'bought' the two German ships and gave them Turkish names, but their German crews and commander remained as before. From his base at Constantinople Souchon attacked Russian ports, with the Turkish

On board the *Goeben*. A visit from the Kaiser. The Turkish flag can be seen

flag flying at his masthead. Although many of the Turks were shocked by this there was nothing they could do about it, and Turkey found herself an ally of Germany for good or ill. Souchon had 'made up their minds' for them by his brilliant dash through the Mediterranean and by the very presence of his powerful ship. The *Goeben* was without doubt the most important vessel of the whole German navy.

Hide and Seek: A German Commerce-raider in the Indian Ocean

Captain Müller of the *Emden* was feeling very pleased with himself. He mused on the futile efforts of the British to trace him. When the war had started he had been with the German China squadron, but had slipped away and sailed into the Indian Ocean. Realizing that the British, French and Russians had a description of his vessel, a fast, light cruiser with three funnels and ten 4·2-in. guns, he had hit on a brilliant deception. He had had a fourth funnel, a dummy, rigged up, and thus from a distance the ship's real identity was concealed.

He remembered the confusion he had caused in the Bay of Bengal when he suddenly appeared and opened fire on cargo vessels. Thirteen ships captured in two weeks! Everyone had raced for safety to nearby Indian ports. The best laugh of all was when they had landed on the British island of Diego Garcia in the middle of the Indian Ocean. The inhabitants did not even know there was a war on, and he and his crew had been welcomed courteously and given every facility to coal and clean the ship. He chuckled as he tried to picture their reaction when eventually they learned how they had been tricked.

Now, replenished and refuelled, he was steaming towards the harbour of Penang on the Malay peninsula, where he understood there were Russian and French destroyers. He had given the order for the dummy funnel to be mounted. The German colours were not to be raised till they were in firing range. He was feeling quite confident in view of his previous successes.

At last the harbour came into view and several vessels could be distinguished. No challenge came as the *Emden* steamed purposefully ahead. Müller singled out the Russian destroyer *Zemchug* as his victim. At just under the mile the German colours were hoisted and a torpedo fired.

The *Zemchug* was caught completely unprepared. With a mighty roar the torpedo struck the rear of the ship. Flames and smoke danced and billowed into the air. Cruising past the blazing wreck the *Emden* opened fire at close range. Then she turned about and released a second torpedo as she passed again on her way out of the harbour. The *Zemchug* was doomed. Fifteen minutes after the *Emden* had fired her first shot the battered victim went down with ninety-one men and officers on board.

As she left the harbour the *Emden* met the unfortunate French destroyer *Mousquet*, which was just returning from patrol. She was blasted almost out of the water in just seven minutes.

Captain Müller had pulled off another lightning raid. He was well satisfied with his day's work. Orders were given to steam south for the Cocos Islands, off north-west Australia. Müller had arranged to meet a collier there. He also hoped to destroy a wireless station on one of the islands. He would not have been so confident had he known what lay ahead for him.

MÜLLER'S LUCK RUNS OUT

News of the *Emden*'s latest exploit was radioed swiftly throughout the world. In the nearby seas all naval personnel were on the alert for the daring German raider. Any unknown four-funnelled vessel would immediately arouse suspicion. When such a ship appeared off the Cocos Islands British telegraph officials scrutinized it carefully. Yes, one funnel was different from the others! Quickly an S.O.S. was tapped out to neighbouring ships.

Müller cruised on into the bay at Cocos Island. Soon he was despatching a landing party to destroy the wireless station. He had no idea of the danger he was in. When smoke appeared on the horizon he took it to be that of the collier he had arranged to meet. Too late! It was H.M.A.S. *Sydney*, two thousand tons heavier, three knots faster and more heavily armed than the *Emden*.

The landing party was abandoned on the island. Quickly

Müller manoeuvred for the expected onslaught. He fired first and made direct hits on the *Sydney*, but the 4-in. shells made little impression on the armour of the Australian cruiser. Soon the *Sydney*'s fire became accurate and deadly. In vain the *Emden* tried to avoid the hail of destruction. Her steering was damaged, her guns were hit, the decks were shattered and torn. Determined not to surrender Müller finally steered his blazing ship on to a coral reef. Even then it required further salvoes from the *Sydney* to make him haul down the German colours and surrender with his surviving crew. With over a third of his crew killed, Captain Müller's exploits had at last ended.

The name *Emden* had become world-famous. As a tribute to his conduct, her captain was allowed to wear his sword, although a prisoner-of-war.

The end of a spectacular career: the battered *Emden*

Battles in the South Seas

While the *Emden* was being sought over thousands of miles of ocean Admiral von Spee with the rest of the German China squadron was heading across the Pacific for South America. On 1 November 1914, he came across Admiral Cradock, cruising off Coronel, on the Chilean coast, with his four ships. Cradock's force was much inferior to that of the Germans, and realizing this he endeavoured to keep the setting sun behind him. Thus the Germans would be dazzled when they opened fire. Von Spee, however, refused to engage until the sun had actually set. He then had perfect targets, for the British ships were silhouetted against the bright western sky. Miles away from the scene of battle was the only ship of Cradock's command which could have redressed the balance: the old battleship *Canopus*, delayed with engine trouble at this vital moment.

Two of the four vessels were lost with all hands, after a gallant but unequal fight. The other two limped home to the Falkland Islands. The bad news was radioed home to London, and the Admiralty hastily despatched what ships it could spare.

Five weeks later the situation was reversed. Von Spee's ships approached the Falkland Islands to raid the British base there, but found to their dismay that very strong British forces had been assembled. In the harbour were the battle-cruisers *Inflexible* and *Invincible*, both modern, fast and carrying 12-in. guns as against the 8·8-in. of the Germans. They had raced south when the news of Coronel became known, on the direct orders of Mr Winston Churchill at the Admiralty. Now began a grim chase of the German squadron. Von Spee in desperation ordered his ships to scatter, but even so all but one were sunk. He himself lost his life; so did his son.

The one ship which escaped was the light cruiser *Dresden*. When this vessel was scuttled by her crew in March 1915, the world's trade routes were freed of German surface ships. After this only the odd daring raider would get past the British patrols. British and French warships of all types were now able to return nearer home, and the Allies could move their war supplies unhindered, save by submarines. When we think of the great variety of raw materials, manufactured goods, machine tools and foodstuffs required by a nation at war we can see that the freedom of the seas was indeed to prove a vital factor in the gaining of final victory.

4 The Land War II: The Eastern Front

The Russian Steamroller Proves a Disappointment

A German officer's experiences at the battle of Tannenberg are described by the one to whom he told the story:

'. . . The sight of thousands of Russians driven into two huge lakes or swamps to drown was ghastly, and the shrieks and cries of the dying men and horses he will never forget. So fearful was the sight of these thousands of men with their guns, horses and ammunition, struggling in the water that, to shorten their agony, they turned the machine-guns on them. But even in spite of that, there was movement seen among them for a week after. And the mowing down of the cavalry brigade at the same time, 500 mounted men on white horses, all killed and packed so closely together that they remained standing. The officer says that this sight was the ghastliest of the whole War.'

At the outbreak of the war great things were expected of the

As the French saw it: a cartoon postcard showing the warring powers of Europe

Russian armies. Many thought that their masses of troops would roll irresistibly forwards into Europe, carrying the war into both Germany and Austria-Hungary. By its very weight the 'Russian Steamroller' would crush all opposition.

It certainly did well in the south, where advancing Austrian forces were sent flying back over their own border, to be pursued for over a hundred miles. But in the north the 'Steamroller' ground to a sharp halt. This was in the part of Germany called East Prussia, a vast countryside of forests, lakes and marshes.

Day by day the Russian army's wireless was monitored. They were not even using code! The German generals Hindenburg and Ludendorff planned their counter-stroke, knowing that what they lacked in numbers would have to be made up in quality and generalship. Light forces were sent to hold one of the two Russian armies in check. The other was enticed into a trap, surrounded and attacked so vigorously that the result was the overwhelming victory for the Germans described above. This was at the hill called Tannenberg.

More was to come. Reinforcements arrived from France, though they could ill be spared, for the Schlieffen Plan was just then reaching its climax. Hindenburg and Ludendorff struck at the other Russian army, further north, by the Masurian Lakes. Germans at home awoke to find thrilling news of yet another startling victory in their morning papers: the Russian invaders were in full retreat, and Prussia was saved!

Breakthrough!

We have already seen how the Germans remained on the defensive on the Western Front throughout most of 1915 (see p. 20). They suffered fewer casualties than their enemies, while the British and French sought again and again for the great breakthrough which somehow they could never find. In the east the position was very different. The armies were spread out more thinly over twice the distance—about seven hundred miles—and the defences were crude and simple compared with those that were appearing on the Western Front. The Russian soldiers were not as well-equipped as either the Austrians or the Germans. The Central Powers had the great advantage of a good railway system to keep their men supplied, whereas the Russian forces which had advanced into Austria found things much more difficult. They had to reload goods at the frontier, for instance, where the gauge of the lines changed.

The Eastern Front

Conrad, the Austrian commander, produced a plan which was taken over by the Germans and put into operation. Around the town of Gorlice, in what is today southern Poland, German and Austrian forces were concentrated. The attack came in May, and the Russian front was first battered and then completely broken. It collapsed on either side of the break-in. The retreat became a rout with Russians surrendering in hordes, or wandering the countryside leaderless and hungry till they were rounded up. Soon the Central Powers were moving forward on a front of five hundred miles. Fortresses fell to their heavy guns. It was Belgium all over again. The ancient city of Warsaw was taken. The cavalry came into its own in the wide, open country, ranging far ahead of the infantry.

It was a terrible time for the weary Russian armies. Often deprived of rest, continually on the retreat, with supplies always doubtful and often completely broken down, it was no wonder that over a quarter of a million men surrendered,

43

The great breakthrough in the East. A German 21-cm. mortar in action against the Russians, August 1915

many of them quite openly rejoicing that, for them, the war was at last over.

With the coming of autumn and winter the advance at last slowed down and halted. Transport had become even more difficult over roads which were far below ordinary European standards. And, yet more important, things were happening in the south which needed attention. Turkey needed help; Serbia was still in the war and had so far proved a match for the Austrians. In October the Germans switched some of their attention to Serbia; Bulgaria joined them. Faced by this new concentration of men the little country, whose proud desire for independence had helped to start it all, was bound to go under. At the dawn of 1916 Serbia was no more, the link between Turkey and Germany had been strengthened, and the Eastern Front had settled down, leaving large areas of Russia in Austrian and German hands. The Central Powers were well content. But if they thought Russia had lost the capacity to hit back, they were badly mistaken.

As in France and Belgium, the tide of war had left its ugly marks on the countryside and peoples of Eastern Europe. The peasants of these parts were not rich at the best of times, but at the end of 1915 they faced the bitterness of winter knowing that bridges and railways had been destroyed, horses, carts and cars commandeered, making trade and supply sluggish and doubtful. Many towns had been bombarded, and homes, shops and public buildings were without roofs or windows in scores of cities. Worse still, in an enormous number of homes, possibly as high as two million, there was mourning for a father, brother or husband who would never return. Even so, the ordeal was not yet over.

The 'All-Highest', the Kaiser, presents Iron Crosses to his soldiers after their Russian victories

45

5 Attack in the East

Gallipoli

Here is a poem written by a British soldier on Turkish soil. It is
about the men he was fighting.

Abdul

We've drunk the boys who rushed the hills
    The men who stormed the beach,
The sappers and the A.S.C.,
    We've had a toast for each;
And the guns and stretcher-bearers—
    But before the bowl is cool,
There's one chap I'd like to mention,
    He's a fellow called ABDUL.

We've heard the twigs a-crackling,
    As we crouched upon our knees,
And his big, black shape went smashing,
    Like a rhino, through the trees.
We've seen him flung in, rank on rank,
    Across the morning sky;
And we've had some pretty shooting,
    And—he knows the way to die.

So though your name be black as ink
    For murder and rapine
Carried out in happy concert
    With your Christians from the Rhine,
We will judge you, Mr Abdul,
    By the test by which *we* can—
That, with all your breath, in life, in death,
    You've played the Gentleman.

A.S.C. stands for Army Service Corps.

You will see from reading the poem that the soldier who
composed it had considerable respect for his Turkish foe. The

newspapers at home gave quite a different picture . . . painting
the Turks as barbarous and inhuman. This difference in attitudes between those at home and those at the fighting fronts
persisted throughout the war.

It seemed a very good idea, early in 1915, to attack Turkey.
The Turks had nothing like the strength of the Germans: perhaps a swift, bold blow at their capital, Constantinople, would
put them out of the war. It would certainly relieve the hard-
pressed Russians, who had asked for help of this sort. Mr
Churchill and Lord Kitchener strongly supported the idea,
and the French promised to help.

The place chosen for the attack was the Gallipoli peninsula,
flanking the vital Dardanelles. The map shows the great importance of the area to both Russia and Turkey.

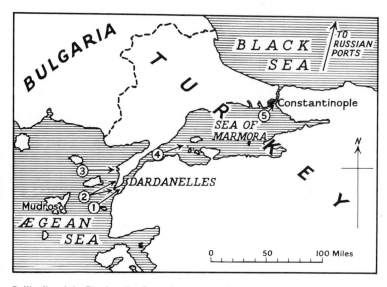

Gallipoli and the Dardanelles. It can be seen that the narrow waterway is the key both
to Constantinople and the ports of the Black Sea. 1 The Attack by the French and
British fleets, 18 March 1915. 2 The Attack by the Armies of Sir Ian Hamilton,
18 April 1915. 3 Landing at Suvla Bay, 7 August 1915. 4 Submarines penetrate the
Straits and do enormous damage. 5 E.11 enters Constantinople harbour, causing a
near-panic.

While the armies were gathering in Egypt a fleet of Allied
warships tried to force its way through to the Turkish capital.

47

On a glorious March morning they advanced purposefully into the Straits. On either side the Turkish forts looked down. Salvo after salvo of huge shells rained on the defences, many of which were soon reduced to rubble and covered with drifting dust and clouds of smoke. The lighter Turkish guns hit the battleships repeatedly, but had little effect against the armour-plate. The thunder of the guns rolled back and forth as the ships forged ahead through the fountains of spray and mist which rose all around.

There seemed every hope of success, but the day was to end less happily. By nightfall the Allied Command was puzzled and disturbed by the loss of three vessels: *Irresistible*, *Ocean*, and the French *Bouvet*. These had been sunk by a row of secretly laid mines, but this was not known till years later.

The crisis point of the whole operation had been reached. The men of the fleets were anxious to push on again the following morning. Commodore Roger Keyes and others with him felt convinced that the enemy was beaten and that a determined attack would carry the fleets through. But the admiral in charge, de Robeck, was full of doubts. Keyes tried to persuade him to press on, and back in London Churchill used the same arguments with the War Cabinet. Both were overruled. The ships were withdrawn, to the great relief of the Turks and their German advisers, for they had indeed been on the verge of defeat.

Five weeks later the armies made their landings. But by this time the enemy was expecting the attack. The Turks had a new commander—the German Liman von Sanders, and he had made the most thorough preparations possible. French, British, Australian and New Zealand troops established themselves on Turkish soil, but did not push very far inland. Back in his battleship headquarters Sir Ian Hamilton was trusting to his local commanders to press forward with the required urgency. But the weather was hot, the country was difficult in the extreme, and the essential thrust did not take place. Instead, the familiar pattern of trench warfare as in France began to appear. Trenches were dug and barbed wire set up. Instead of advancing rapidly to Constantinople the troops found themselves pinned to a small part of the peninsula.

The summer of 1915 saw both Allies and enemy in deadlock.

The soldiers lived .a strange life in their rough trenches and shelters, always within range of the Turkish artillery. They had plenty of food, but it was very monotonous—mainly jam, biscuits and 'bully-beef'. Insects plagued them throughout the sultry summer weather, and it was impossible to open tinned food without its being instantly covered with flies. Many caught dysentery and had to be taken off in hospital ships. Water was rationed, being brought in by the Navy and carried by mule to the different units. At one point men of the Australian and New Zealand Army Corps found themselves clinging to the area surrounding a small bay, which became known as 'Anzac' Cove. Their front-line trenches were murderously close to the enemy—barely ten yards in some cases.

Anzac Cove. Dugouts and shelters can be seen, crowded together on the cliffs

One part of the Allied plans met with great success. This was a submarine offensive through the Dardanelles. British and French commanders brought their boats again and again through the minefields and nets, and once in the Sea of Marmora did enormous damage. Warships, troopships and merchant vessels were sunk one after the other and in such numbers that the Turkish war effort was seriously affected. Ships actually in the harbour at Constantinople were attacked, railway lines blown up by raiding parties, and shore buildings bombarded.

49

The 'E.11': A Dangerous Mission Under Water

One such submarine was the *E.11*, under Captain Nasmith.
This vessel penetrated fourteen rows of minefields, anti-sub-
marine nets, floating mines, depth charges, and shore batteries
to carry out its mission of damage in Constantinople Harbour.
Bill Wheeler, a member of the crew has described his experiences:

'Every time we were about to go into action Captain Nasmith had every man who could be spared forward under the
conning tower for prayers. It was a strange occasion, some 50
feet below the surface. But we all appreciated the gravity of the
situation. Every boat was our enemy and we could take no
chances. Even the innocent-looking fishing vessels were dealt
with—by surfacing underneath them.

'We made three successful trips into the Sea of Marmora.
Conditions were very cramped below. Our daily rations were
one pint of water, three sea biscuits and a tin of corned beef
(we called it bully-beef). There were no bunks and sleeping on
the floor could be rather uncomfortable, especially when the
condensation dripped from the roof and splashed one's face.

'Looking back it seems incredible that we actually survived
those missions. I can still remember the closest shave we had.
It was in Constantinople Harbour, where we had just sunk an
ammunition ship with a tin-fish (torpedo). The harbour guns
opened up. Right on the bottom we sat, engines stopped, no
lights, and our oxygen supply getting lower. We could not
move until the bombardment around us ceased. Finally we
got away by scraping along the bottom underneath the anti-
submarine nets. Even then the danger had not passed: for later
on after negotiating a minefield we discovered to our horror
that a mine had become entangled with us and we were towing
it along. There it was—swinging about like a toy balloon,
threatening at any moment to bang into the side and . . . !
To shake it off we dived as swiftly as possible, cut the motors
and started up full astern. That did the trick. It sounds easy
now, of course, but to us at the time, cooped up in that mass of
machinery, we felt that we had reached the end of the road
when we first saw that black monster dancing around us.'

E.11 returns from her patrol in the Sea of Marmora. She is cheered by the crew of H.M.S. *Grampus*

Meanwhile it had become obvious that the first plan of an attack on Constantinople had failed. The armies were in a difficult position. In October 1915 a new commander was appointed, and he very quickly decided to withdraw all the forces. After elaborate preparations the Allied armies were removed from Gallipoli on two remarkable nights. The second of these was that of 8 January 1916, when 17,000 men were embarked. They left their positions deserted, but the Turks suspected nothing. Only the previous night a Turkish attack had been repulsed with great slaughter, and the enemy did not imagine the end of the campaign was so near. Ingenious devices left in the trenches kept up occasional rifle-fire throughout the night, although the men had crept away hours before.

The Turks made much of this invasion which failed. Constantinople was safe. Churchill was disgraced, for the time being. The Allies' short cut to victory in the east had proved hard and difficult after all. But for a few hours, on 18 March, it had been 'touch and go'.

6 The War at Sea II

The Most Important Ships of the War: 2 The British 'Lusitania' 7 May 1915

It was a calm but hazy afternoon as the great British liner *Lusitania* approached the Irish Sea bound for Liverpool from New York. On board were some 2,000 passengers and crew, including many Americans, whose country was not then in the war. The crew went about their duties. The passengers were relaxing after lunch. Children were playing on the boat deck. The watch scanned the seas for any unusual objects: since the Germans had started their U-boat campaign all ships were proceeding with extra care.

Suddenly the cry went up: 'Submarine to starboard!' The order was given to turn about, but before anything could be done the torpedo had been fired and was speeding towards the great liner, leaving an angry foam wash behind it. There was a tremendous explosion and a great hole was torn in the ship's side. Water cascaded into the hold and the engine rooms. The ship began to list badly.

'Abandon ship! Lower the boats!' The crew hurriedly assisted the women and children to put on their life-jackets, and hustled them to the lifeboats. Anxious fathers waved to their wives and children from the sloping decks as the first boats were lowered. The radio operator tapped out an urgent S.O.S. message to all neighbouring vessels. The ship lurched and began to keel over on to its side, preventing the launching of any more of the boats. Screaming women and children milled together with the crew, trying to hold their balance on the sloping decks, which in parts were already beneath the water.

'Jump for your lives! She's going under!' Mortally wounded, the great liner heaved over and plunged below the waves, carrying to their deaths over 1,000 men, women and children. Only a few survived the catastrophe and were eventually picked up to tell their tragic stories.

The news of sinkings like that of the *Lusitania* caused great bitterness in the United States, and angry notes were exchanged with Germany. The way was being prepared for the United States to enter the war, though for another two years she would still keep up her neutrality.

The Battle of Jutland, 31 May 1916

The Battle-Cruiser Fleet and the Light Cruiser Squadron, Flagship H.M.S. *Galatea*, were on a sweep of the North Sea in search of German submarines and warships. Not far away were the great battleships of Admiral Jellicoe, engaged in a similar task. Throughout the long night and into the following day the search went on, but as usual there were no Germans to be seen.

The afternoon of 31 May was warm and sunny, and the *Galatea*'s wireless officer was basking in the sun on the quarter-deck. He had been through these sweeps before—many times—but nothing ever happened. In fact, he was rather bored by the whole proceeding. As he listened to the water lapping on the hull the war seemed far away.

Even when the bugle sounded 'Action Stations' he was not unduly worried. He hauled himself up and strolled along to the ladder which led down to his wireless cabin. It was quite normal to carry out the drill for action while on a sweep. 'Keeps one occupied, I suppose', he mused. 'Anyway nothing ever hap . . .'

Boommm! He almost fell down the ladder on to his back, dazed and deafened. The fo'c'sle 6-in. gun had been fired . . . just above his head! He scrambled up quickly and dived into his cabin just in time to see a message come rattling down the tube from the bridge. 'Enemy in sight, consisting of one destroyer.'

'This is it', he thought excitedly as he transmitted the message to all neighbouring vessels. Soon more and more German ships were sighted—destroyers, cruisers, battleships. The air resounded to the whine of shells. The great battle of Jutland was on. 250 warships, including fifty battleships, were racing into action at high speed.

THE END OF A BATTLE-CRUISER

Petty Officer Francis, of H.M.S. *Queen Mary*, paused from the task of supervising the loading of the 13-in. turret guns and mopped his brow. All around him in the turret there was noise and bustle as the great guns were loaded and reloaded with shells. It was now one and a half hours since the first shots had been fired, and everyone was working at full speed to keep up the rain of destruction on the German warships ahead. Now and again he felt the ship lurch as though it had been struck; but no-one panicked and everyone carried on with his duties.

He seized a moment to look through the turret periscope. What he saw he did not like. The whole of the 4-in. battery to the rear of the ship was smashed to pieces. Beyond the ship, about half a mile away, H.M.S. *Indefatigable* was limping out of line with black smoke billowing from her side.

When he turned away several anxious faces were watching him. They read his thoughts. The Germans now had the range of their ship. It would not be long before a direct hit would be scored upon them. He pressed his lips together and rapped out the orders to load up the guns again. He was determined to fire away every shell he had before the enemy fired the fatal shot.

It was not long delayed. There was continuous, crashing roar about his ears. A great bulge erupted in the turret floor. Everything went suddenly blank.

'What's that? Water? I can hear water trickling . . . And everywhere's so quiet . . . Tommy! Is that you?'

'Come on, Sir. Let's get out. We're all smashed up here.'

'What about the others? Smithy . . . Taffy?'

'Come on, Sir. Gun dropped on them, poor blighters.'

'Dead? . . . Everywhere's so quiet . . . like being in a church.'

'Up you come. Try and make the ladder. That's it. Slowly . . . mind your head. That's it.'

'God . . . Tommy, what a mess. Everything's shattered.'

'She's listing, Sir. Going under.'

'There's number three turret. Hey, you chaps . . . anyone for a swim? We'd better get off before she goes down. Good luck!'

'Good luck, Sir!'

A small group of men walked off the sinking ship into the cold waters of the North Sea. Wearily they began swimming away from the stricken vessel. Francis had nearly covered fifty yards when he heard the explosion, and was showered with debris and flying pieces. Instinctively he submerged, holding his breath, and eventually gained the surface clinging to a floating spar. The ship was gone, and the surface of the water was covered with its scattered fragments. An enormous pall of smoke rose high into the air.

He could not see his companions. He found it difficult to see at all. Floating oil clogged his eyes and made them sting. He began to feel sick. He clung to the spar for ages, or so it seemed, before he was hailed by a passing destroyer and hauled up on a line. Afterwards he remembered the leather settee, his eyes being bathed, the explosions, the reassuring voices, the whine of shells, the motion of the ship. . . .

Petty Officer Francis was one of the lucky few who survived the explosion of the *Queen Mary*. Indeed, he was twice lucky. Several of the men who were attending him on board the British destroyer *Petard* were killed when a shell crashed into the cabin where he lay, leaving him untouched.

A remarkable photograph, taken during the battle. H.M.S. *Queen Mary* has just blown up

55

Meanwhile, there was plenty of excitement elsewhere.

There was the hair-raising incident some hours later, when men on board the *Spitfire* watched a blazing ship steaming towards them out of the night. It seemed inevitable that a collision would occur, but the doomed vessel missed them by a few feet, the heat of the flames being felt quite fiercely on board. On into the darkness forged the unfortunate ship, and some time later a muffled explosion came from the direction it had taken. Then again, H.M.S. *Sparrowhawk*, damaged in collision, was drifting helplessly in the early morning mist when the huge shape of a German cruiser loomed up. All tensed themselves fearfully for the dreadful salvo they expected, but to their amazement and great relief the vessel ignored them and disappeared into the mist.

The story of John Travers Cornwell lends heart to all schoolboys. Hardly sixteen, he had taken up his post by his gun aboard H.M.S. *Chester* early in the action and was quickly passing on the orders that were being relayed to him. Wounded by a fateful shell, he still remained at his post awaiting further orders despite the fact that all his companions lay dead around him. He died later of his injuries, and of him his Captain said: 'His devotion to duty was an example to all of us. . . . He stayed there, waiting under heavy fire with just his own brave heart and God's help to support him.' He was posthumously awarded the Victoria Cross, and members of the Boy Scout movement will know that Scouting's highest award for gallantry is named after him.

Stories like these merely convey a slight impression of the events at Jutland. There were thousands, some heroic, some sad; some British, some German. The survivors came away with memories of screeching shells, violent explosions, sudden searchlights in the night and hours spent with eyes straining into the darkness, where somewhere, out ahead, was the German High Seas Fleet. Ships met in the night, momentarily not knowing one another for either friend or foe. But when morning came the German fleet had disappeared back to its bases.

The British claimed a victory, for their fleet still dominated the seas, and their enemy had fled. The Germans also claimed a victory, for they had lost fewer ships and fewer men. What were the facts?

John Travers Cornwell, the boy V.C., killed at Jutland

Cornwell's last letter home

Most important, is that the two battle-fleets, with their heavily armoured dreadnoughts, had been in action with one another for less than a quarter of an hour, due to Jellicoe's caution.

The battle-cruisers had borne the brunt of the fighting. Beatty had handled them well. But a serious weakness had been revealed: a liability to blow up when hit by plunging shells at great range. *Indefatigable*, *Invincible* and *Queen Mary* had been lost in this way. The battle-cruiser *Lion* had only been saved from a similar end when her magazines had been flooded in the nick of time.

There had been no lack of bravery on either side. But for the Germans a full-scale battle between the dreadnoughts would have been disastrous. The overwhelming strength of the Grand Fleet forbade it. They were right to refuse action when Jellicoe appeared, and fortunate that they were able to crash through the lighter forces of the British rearguard on the way home, during darkness.

The Battle of Jutland did not vitally alter the war at sea. The Entente was still just as supreme on the oceans of the world. Germany's best hope lay with the submarine. She switched her greatest efforts to building and manning them in ever-larger numbers.

Many at home blamed Jellicoe for not bringing on a great battle of annihilation between the two fleets, as Nelson had done at Trafalgar. His command of the Grand Fleet was given to Beatty six months after Jutland, and certainly Beatty seemed to have more of the 'Nelson Touch'. But we should remember that Jellicoe in 1916 bore a terrible responsibility: to lose his fleet, or even a part of it, would have meant losing the war; whereas a great victory would have had nothing like the same effect on the Germans. In 1917 Beatty too became cautious.

A Short Cut to Victory: The U-boats Strike their Blow

The U-boats of the German navy, unlike the High Seas Fleet, were constantly at sea in all weathers. From their home bases and from captured Belgian harbours they scoured the North Sea and penetrated the English Channel to prey on shipping. Entente losses mounted as the number of U-boats steadily increased. Concentrated in the crowded shipping lanes which led to the great British and French ports, they were a growing menace to the Allies.

By day the U-boats passing down the Channel to their patrol stations would do so below the surface, for destroyer and motor-boat patrols were constantly active. At night they would make better speed on the surface, trusting to the darkness to hide them from their enemies. Even so, the most careful watch was always necessary, for to be caught by the stabbing glare of a warship's searchlight might easily prove fatal.

Powerful batteries supplied the electricity to run the vessel when submerged. But once below the waves its endurance had very definite limits. The batteries would need recharging, and this meant coming to the surface to use the diesel engines.

The crews lived in a state of tension and anxiety, often concealed by youthful high spirits. They lived in confined, cramped quarters, amid all sorts of machinery and instruments. They were the most active seamen of the Kaiser's navy, and in 1917 were to bring Germany nearer to victory than at any time since the battle of the Marne.

The men who almost brought victory. U-boat men in the torpedo room of their submarine

'SINK AT SIGHT'

Von Tirpitz and other German admirals believed that the submarine war could bring a rapid victory for Germany. But to have this effect, all ships found approaching Britain or France would have to be sunk as soon as seen, even if owned by neutral countries. Britain's vital trade would be sent to the bottom, or at least terrorized off the seas; the British would thus receive their death-blow as a nation at war. The admirals guaranteed that they could bring this about within a few weeks: six months at the very outside.

Bethmann-Hollweg and other German leaders hesitated; for an all-out submarine war would turn the United States against them, and this they had hoped to avoid. But the prize of a quick victory lured them on. On 31 January 1917, the admirals had their way. U-boats were ordered to sink at sight all ships found within the war zone around Britain, France and Italy.

The result shook Britain almost to the point of defeat. Losses increased immediately, and food stocks in Britain dwindled in the most alarming way. March and April saw over six hundred merchant ships fall to the U-boats. If an answer could not be found, and quickly, Britain would have to ask for peace. To avoid alarm the public was not told the true facts.

A steamer is sunk by torpedo. In this case the submarine had surfaced. The wake of the torpedo is visible

In the nick of time the convoy system was devised and put into operation on the direct orders of the Prime Minister, Mr Lloyd George. Merchantmen sailed together in groups with naval escorts. Many had feared this would lead to worse losses than ever, and so numbers of sinkings were watched anxiously. By the end of the year it was clear that the U-boats were being mastered, though their toll was still a heavy one.

During 1918 Admiral Roger Keyes was in charge at Dover, and the defences across the Channel became formidable. Flare-ships made the darkest night as bright as day; searchlights swept the surface of the sea; motor-boats, sloops, armed trawlers and destroyers kept up a constant patrol. The U-boat forced to dive ran the risk of hitting one of the deep-laid mines. The peril became so great that the larger U-boats were forced to take the northern route to the Atlantic round Scotland, and thus valuable days were lost in passage to and from the patrol areas.

ZEEBRUGGE

Roger Keyes was determined to do yet more to check the U-boats. He led a task force to the Flanders ports of Zeebrugge and Ostend, which were in use by the smaller submarines. In one of the most daring attacks of the war the harbour at Zeebrugge was entered and the defences engaged by marines. Three old warships, filled with concrete, approached the narrow channel which led to the U-boats' lair. Two were sunk right across the deep channel, and the third nearby. Although later it was found that the raid had had less effect on U-boat movements than had been hoped, whilst that at Ostend had failed, all Britain was thrilled by the bravery shown, and the signal sent by the daring Keyes to his marines and sailors, 'St George for England!', became famous, for the attack was made on St George's Day, 23 April. Ostend was successfully blocked a few days later.

7 The World-Wide Conflict

Africa, and the Genius of Lettow-Vorbeck

The plight of the German colonies was hopeless from the first, since they were cut off from home. Those in the Pacific had fallen early, but Africa was a more difficult proposition. The four German colonies were Togoland, Cameroon, German South West Africa and German East Africa.

The first three had been conquered by the end of 1915, despite the great difficulties of campaigning in such areas, where troops had to be moved hundreds of miles through arid or tropical country. The Union of South Africa dealt with German South West Africa. The troops were led by General Botha, who only fifteen years previously had been a bitter opponent of the British in the Boer War. The main problems encountered were those of keeping up a supply of fresh water for troops and animals, and of fighting the deadly tropical diseases.

German East Africa became Tanganyika, and is now Tanzania. Here the presence of one man, Colonel von Lettow-Vorbeck, made a great deal of difference. He organized his few German and his native soldiers so effectively that they defied all attempts to capture or destroy them. Early attacks on the German colony were repulsed or petered out. Lettow-Vorbeck fought when he was in a strong position, but when in 1916 he was faced by very superior forces under General Smuts, his men retreated or melted away into the deep bush country, to re-form again elsewhere. The northern half of the colony was slowly taken, even so.

Back in Europe, admiration for the achievements of Lettow-Vorbeck was strong. His position was improved temporarily when a blockade runner managed to get through the patrols to bring much-needed ammunition and supplies from home. Another interesting effort was made to supply him by

Zeppelin, and the huge machine crossed the Mediterranean and much of North Africa before being recalled by mistake.

STRANGE SIGHTS IN THE JUNGLE

On Lake Tanganyika the Germans had a number of vessels with which they controlled the great lake and the shore towns. How could the Allied forces—British, French, Belgian or, later, Portuguese—deal with them? Mimi and Tou-Tou were the answers.

These were two armed motor-boats sent out from England in the summer of 1915. They went by rail from Cape Town into Rhodesia. Then the railway came to an end, and traction engines took over. Through tough bush country and across rivers, along tracks which normally never saw any mechanized transport, the two boats were pulled by the heavy engines, coughing and puffing as they forged along. Many a native village saw such a sight for the first time, and the people turned out to watch.

Overland to Lake Tanganyika. A traction engine forges ahead with one of the armed motor-boats

The effort was well worthwhile. The boats were launched on the lake and soon dominated it. The German vessels, steamers and a small gunboat, were soon either sunk or surrendered.

Lettow-Vorbeck was eventually thrust out of Tanganyika. He crossed into Portuguese Mozambique, taking his now much diminished force of Germans and askaris with him. He was still at large on 11 November 1918, and did not hear the news of the end of the war for some days. He then surrendered, having put up a fight with limited resources which had stirred the imagination of the world, and which had held down large Allied forces throughout the period of the war—well over four years.

The Cloud-Fighters: Italy Joins the War

'Picture to yourself my men, 9,000 feet up in the clouds for seven months, in deep snow, so close to the Austrians that at some points the men can see their enemies' eyes through the observation holes. Imagine the difficulties of such life with continual sniping and bomb-throwing. . . .' Thus King Victor Emmanuel III of Italy described the conditions under which the Italians were fighting in the Alps on their frontier with Austria. Of course these words applied equally well to the Austrians whom they faced.

When the war broke out in 1914, Italy had been an ally of Austria and Germany, the third member of the Triple Alliance (see p. 5). But the Italians had refused to take the side of Austria in the quarrel with Serbia and declared their intention of remaining neutral. As the war dragged out, however, some Italians felt that they might obtain some advantages from it. They had long wished that their ally Austria would give up to Italy some border lands which they felt were rightly theirs: the Trentino, the South Tyrol, and the coastline around Trieste (see map). When the Austrians refused to agree to this all the old Italian hatred for their former enemy flared up and they broke away from the Triple Alliance. Soon afterwards, on 23 May 1915, Italy declared war on Austria, having previously agreed secretly with the Entente Powers in the Treaty of London to co-operate with them against all their enemies.

Thus the Italians turned their faces northwards, towards the great towering peaks of the Alps, the frontier with Austria.

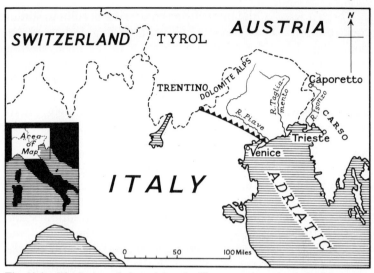

The Alpine War between Italy and Austria. The mountainous borderlands saw some of the most difficult conditions encountered during the war. The toothed line shows how far the Italians were pushed back after Caporetto

'PERIL ON THE PEAKS'

Pietro started. In the hot stuffy atmosphere of the tiny dugout he found it difficult to stay awake. He peered through the narrow vents of the iron-plated wall. A heat haze shimmered across the parched, dusty hillside. Below him the hillside fell away sharply, almost precipitously, to the greener wooded slopes on the valley floor. There was little sign of any movement. There rarely was in the heat of the day. Out there the exposed barrel of a rifle would become unbearably hot in a very short time.

A muffled 'boom' sounded from across the other side, echoing mockingly along the brittle-baked slabs. He listened anxiously for the explosion, and tensed as the shell whizzed somewhere overhead to explode violently farther up the mountain. Now came the real strain . . . he held his breath waiting for the telltale rattle and clatter that signified the roll of shattered rock fragments. He shuddered as he recalled the injuries which he had seen those flying fragments inflict on exposed soldiers. But then he was little better off where he was. It was not uncommon for men to be entombed by rockfalls set in motion by reverberating explosions.

65

There it was . . . the intermittent pattering of rolling, sliding rock-splinters. That heavy, hollow thudding indicated the bounding of boulders. He flung himself to the floor, steeling himself for the terrible blow. . . . It came . . . and it went . . . he raised himself slowly. He was still alive! Thankfully he groped for the water flask. It was empty! He settled down again to his watching position. It was going to be a long, thirsty afternoon until the relief came at dusk.

MAN AGAINST MAN: MAN AGAINST NATURE

Pietro's story gives an indication of the type of problem which faced the Italians and the Austrians waging their war in the Alps. As far as Italy was concerned, there were three hazards to be overcome: one was the task of dragging supplies and heavy artillery up the steep, broken terrain; the second was the weather, both in winter and summer; and the third was the fact that the Austrians controlled all the high mountain passes and therefore were able to dominate the ascending Italians with their heavy siege guns.

SUPPLIES: DIZZY HEIGHTS AND WIREWAYS

Where possible narrow, twisting roads forged their way, ribbon-like, up towards the towering mountain peaks. From hill to hill and ridge to ridge steel cables were slung, spanning the great depths of the valleys and overlooking yawning chasms. Up these 'wireways' food, water, ammunition, timber and metal-sheet (for gun entrenchments) were sent. Down them came the wounded and the lame. It must have required

A wounded man is removed by cable from the scene of fighting

strong nerves to be ferried on one of these cables when one remembers that below lay sometimes a drop of hundreds of feet. Often they would be shrouded in the clouds and the atmosphere would be damp and eerie.

The heavy siege guns were the greatest difficulty. Some of these were hauled up the wireways, no doubt swinging dangerously. With others it was necessary for hundreds of men to spend many sweating hours and days pulling them up the rough, broken slopes. Nevertheless, many of these were successfully mounted above the snow line and thundered out from peaks above 9,000 feet . . . quite an achievement when one considers their bulk and weight.

War above the snow line: an Alpine shelter

FROM DESERT HEAT TO ARCTIC COLD

The summer campaigns in the Isonzo region and in the Dolomites were dusty, thirsty affairs. The Isonzo in parts was not unlike the great deserts of the world, arid and parched, sunbaked and hazy. In such places the water carts were never far from the front line. The Carso was a hot, boulder-strewn plateau, normally inhabited only by lizards.

Higher up the mountains snow and frost were enemies for the greater part of the year. On the steep, snow-covered slopes concentrations of troops were not possible. There the soldiers fought in small groups—the Alpini regiments. They were skilled mountaineers who sought the enemy across treacherous glaciers and along rugged, vertical cliffs. Both sides were at the mercy of gale and storm. It was not unusual for parties to disappear without trace . . . the victims perhaps of avalanches. The melting spring snows revealed many a preserved, frozen corpse, Nature's grim reminder of the respect she demanded. Often enveloped in mist for days on end, the 'cloud-fighters', as they were called, waged a war very different from that experienced on the Western Front.

CAPORETTO: THE GREAT ITALIAN DISASTER

During the first two years of their fighting the Italians made several attempts to dislodge the Austrians from their entrenched positions in the north, but without success. Although both sides achieved minor victories, sometimes involving high losses, the overall pattern of the Front remained the same: the Austrians used their strategic position well—every Italian attack was uphill.

By 1917 there was considerable disillusionment in the Italian ranks. They had joined the war with great enthusiasm but so far their sacrifices had not been rewarded. Enemy propaganda leaflets, dropped from the sky, fanned the discontent. The Pope came out against the dreadful slaughter. Some people felt that the British and the French were unwilling to transfer men and materials from the Western Front. This very idea had in fact been discussed early in 1917, but had finally been rejected in favour of yet a further attempt on the Western Front. This decision proved fateful to the Italian armies in the autumn of 1917. The promise of some contributions of heavy artillery did not improve the morale of the already shaken soldiers. And worse still, General Cadorna feared that the Germans were planning to send troops to support the Austrians. These fears turned out to be true.

In September of 1917 the Germans, anticipating the defeat

of the Russians in the east, transferred to Italy seven divisions with artillery support. A joint Austrian-German drive was to be launched. All was mounted for 25 October, a foggy, rainy, and in places even snowy, morning.

When the attack came utter confusion reigned in the Italian ranks. Communications broke down and the prevailing misty conditions shrouded the whole affair in chaos. No emergency communication system had been prepared for this kind of breakdown, with the result that orders could not be transmitted nor information relayed on the movements of the enemy. The Austrians and the Germans rolled straight through the front lines. Little resistance was made. Whole trench garrisons surrendered on the spot while others turned tail and fled. Weapons were cast aside in the frenzied race to escape the encircling, advancing armies. The news that there were Germans with the Austrians spread panic wherever it reached. There were instances recorded of Italians deserting to the Austrians shouting 'Long Live Austria' and 'On to Rome'.

At the River Tagliamento an attempt was made to stem the incredible tide, but without success: on swept the Central Powers. In just over a week they covered seventy miles! Indeed, they had hardly expected to be so successful themselves and by the time they reached the River Piave their supply lines were becoming strained. At the Piave the Italians stood, now fortified with British and French troops transferred hastily to prevent a complete Italian rout. But the damage had been done. The Italians had lost a quarter of a million men, mostly prisoners, and innumerable guns, supplies, horses, transport vehicles, as well as food stocks. Worse still, in future the Allies would have to support the Italians constantly. In the face of the crack German divisions the Italians had proved very much a paper army.

Lloyd George, the British Prime Minister at the time, has said this:

'Let us put ourselves in the plight of the sensitive and imaginative Italian soldier at and after Caporetto. To him the German warrior was a creature of report. The Germans had not hitherto appeared on the Italian front and the Italian soldiers knew nothing of his measure as a fighter. . . . All he knew about the German was that he had overrun Belgium in a fortnight; that he had conquered the richest provinces of France, driving the great army of France and the picked troops of England pell-mell almost to the gates of Paris; that the combined efforts of England and France had failed to tear the captured land free . . . ; that while Germany was doing all this with her right arm, with her left she had smashed Russia, Roumania and Serbia. Having accomplished their destruction she was now sending her triumphant legions down to the Italian valleys against an army with not one-tenth the equipment of the British or French. No wonder the stoutest Italian soldier felt a shiver of apprehension.'

In spite of this generous appraisal Caporetto overshadowed all the later Italian campaigns. Nothing it seemed could shake off the dreadful reversal. Italians felt it had been a mistake to join the war at all. Later, at the peace conference, their dissatisfaction increased, and they claimed they had not been fairly rewarded for their sacrifices. The war left them discontented, disillusioned and unhappy.

Japan Joins the War in the Far East

On 9 November 1914, the following item appeared in the German official war news:

'Woe to you, Japan! England has betrayed the white races in the surrender of Tsing Tau to the Japanese. There is no honour for England or Japan in having taken Tsing Tau, which was defended by only 6,000 Germans, with tenfold superiority after ten weeks' siege. The day of reckoning with Japan will probably be long postponed. Our mills here must grind slowly, but our time will come.'

It is obvious from these bitter comments that the Japanese assistance to the Entente Powers in the Far East had struck the Germans a severe blow. The Germans had been powerless to prevent their island colonies in the Pacific, the Marianas, the Carolines and the Marshalls from falling to the Japanese navy. Admiral von Spee had chosen to cross the Pacific Ocean in order to avoid their naval patrols, and you will remember that this led to the battles in the South Seas (see p. 39).

But the fortress of Tsing Tau, guarding the harbour of Kiao-chow, put up sharp resistance to the attacking forces. The Germans were proud of their 'model settlement', as the

Kaiser called Kiao-chow, and the defenders rallied to 'do their duty to the last'. They knew that no help could reach them from Europe and that therefore all supplies were strictly limited. Nevertheless, they ignored the Japanese ultimatum which called on them to evacuate the fort.

The month of September must have been quite a nerve-racking time to the trapped men within the fortress. All around them they could see the preparations which were being made for their destruction. Great siege guns were dragged up the surrounding hillsides where they could dominate the doomed city. One by one they saw their neighbouring smaller fortresses fall to the encircling enemy. Finally, when all was ready, 22,000 Japanese troops, with 1,750 British supporting, focused their sights on Tsing Tau.

On 29 October there began a general bombardment by land and by sea. It was a hopeless task for the defenders, who were soon hampered by their serious lack of ammunition. The Japanese soldiers pushed ever nearer. By 6 November, they had dug trenches within twenty-five yards of the German defences. The end was in sight. As the Japanese victoriously

A Japanese poster depicting the capture of Tsing Tau from the Germans

climbed the last few yards up the Bismarck slope they were greeted by tremendous explosions as the Germans used what was left of their ammunition to destroy their guns and defences. They then surrendered to their conquerors unconditionally. Their defeat saw the end of the German Empire in Asia, and great were the laments of the Germans at home. 'Woe to you, Japan!'

Throughout the remainder of the War the Japanese continued to provide assistance to the Entente Powers, especially by escorting troopships, sometimes as far as the Mediterranean. But they steadfastly refused to involve themselves in the trench warfare on the Western Front. That to them was a European affair, and their concern was the Far East and the Pacific. Despite the fact that they went on to replace the Germans as the Great Power in the Pacific and began to pursue unwelcome policies in China, Japan's assistance was valuable in ending the German Empire in the Far East. What Japan would do with her increased power in the East remained a question for the future.

The United States Joins the Allies

On 2 April 1917, Woodrow Wilson, President of the United States, was on his way to the Capitol in Washington to address a special meeting of Congress. He went with a sad heart, but a mind at last made up. He had struggled hard to keep the United States out of the furious conflict which had raged so terribly since 1914. In the Presidential election of 1916 he had been re-elected as 'the man who kept us out of war'. But in the spring of 1917 there was no longer any hope of staying neutral.

Americans had been horrified enough at the torpedoing of the *Lusitania*, nearly two years before, but after all she was a British ship; the new 'sink at sight' campaign of the U-boats was now claiming American victims—already six ships had been sunk in six weeks. Many captains were afraid to take their ships to European ports, knowing that as soon as they entered the 'war zone' they might become a target for a torpedo at any minute. American protests had been brushed aside.

A month after the ruthless U-boat war had begun, the American papers had carried startling news which had changed opinions and attitudes almost overnight. Many had refused to believe that Germany had any hostility towards the United States, but on 1 March the text of an amazing telegram was printed for all to read. In it the German Foreign Minister offered American territory to Mexico as a bribe to bring her into the war on the German side. The American mood had immediately become one of rage and hostility, especially when Zimmermann, the German Foreign Minister, had admitted that the telegram was genuine. Here was a German actually proposing to the Mexicans that they should together 'slice up' the United States! War had become inevitable.

The audience awaiting the President at the Capitol was composed of Representatives, Senators, diplomats, pressmen and members of the Supreme Court of the United States. It was an historic occasion, for the United States was about to abandon her policy of avoiding entanglements with the European powers, a policy which had been advised originally to the young republic by George Washington, well over a century previously.

There was complete silence as the President spoke. He said that the policies of the Imperial German Government made it impossible for the United States not to enter the war:

'Vessels of every kind, whatever their flag, their character, their cargo, their destination, their errand, have been ruthlessly sent to the bottom without warning and without thought of help or mercy for those on board, the vessels of friendly neutrals along with those of belligerents. . . . The world must be made safe for democracy. . . .'

In a reference to the Zimmermann telegram he said that the German Government 'means to stir up enemies against us at our very doors'. He asked Congress to declare war. The roar of enthusiasm at the end of his address was echoed by the whole nation.

The Entente Powers were profoundly relieved. American strength was a guarantee of victory, eventually. But it would be many months before an American army could be enlisted, trained, transported to France and brought into action. As time went on it became plain that the Russian collapse would mean that the Germans would switch their troops from the East to France. The heaviest attacks of the war were certain to follow, and the brunt of these must be borne by the French and British. On the seas, however, it was different: American merchant and naval ships played a large part in the war at sea right from the first, reinforcing the British Grand Fleet and providing much-needed escorts for the convoys which were soon plying in the Atlantic.

The most important effect of the American entry was on the morale of the fighting powers. Allied soldiers were cheered as they thought of the American legions who would soon be joining them in ever-increasing numbers in the battlefields of France; German soldiers found yet another mighty enemy arrayed against them, and one whom they could not hope to strike in his homeland. For them, it must be victory soon, or never.

The Turkish Empire in Retreat

The Turkish Empire of 1914 included the modern states of Syria, Jordan, Israel and Iraq. At the outer fringes of this empire lay the Suez Canal and the oil-exporting centre of Abadan, at the head of the Persian Gulf. Both were of the greatest importance to the British Empire. The grip on Egypt, already in British hands, was tightened, and Abadan was captured early in the war. Even so the British were badly shaken by Turkish successes in both areas in 1915. But the danger passed, and the British armies were strengthened.

By 1917 the Turks were on the defensive, and their Empire in the East began to shrink under attack from British, Indian, Australian and New Zealand forces.

It was gruelling work in a hot climate, where disease could sometimes hit as hard as the enemy. Water was precious and rationed, being required for thousands of horses and camels as well as men. Good roads were rare. In Mesopotamia the rivers Tigris and Euphrates were used as highways, with supply boats constantly going up and down. Across the stretch of arid country between Egypt and Palestine a railway and a water pipeline were constructed.

The Turks faced an enemy who was better equipped and in larger numbers, and who also possessed many more aircraft. Despite the help of German airmen and gunners, and the

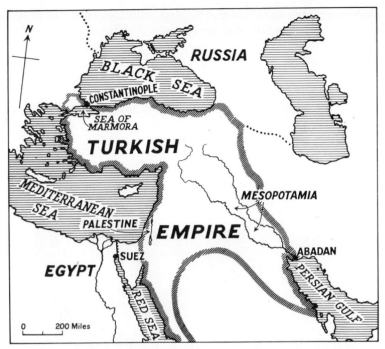

The Turkish Empire of 1914. It stretched from Europe to the Indian Ocean

advice of German generals, they were forced steadily back. The delighted British public read, month after month, of the capture of cities with ancient and famous names—Bagdad, Jerusalem, Damascus and Antioch among them.

As they struggled to retain their hold on Palestine and Syria, the Turks found themselves threatened from the rear. Many of the Arab tribes hated them, and found an Englishman who led them in a series of devastating raids. He was the famous Lawrence of Arabia, who had a remarkable gift of leadership. He shared the life of his tough, hard-riding warriors in the desert, and they struck at the Turkish garrisons and railways behind the fighting fronts, cutting off supplies and causing havoc wherever they turned up, unexpectedly, out of the waste and desert lands the Arabs knew so well.

By the end of war Palestine, Syria and Mesopotamia were lost to the Turkish Empire for good, and the Arabs found

75

themselves free at last of the masters who had ruled them for the previous three or four centuries.

11 December 1917. General Sir Edmund Allenby enters Jerusalem. The news of its capture was a tonic for the war-tired people of Britain

Russia in Revolution

THE STEAMROLLER AGAIN: BRUSILOV GETS MOVING

After the great defeats and disasters of 1915 the Russian steam-roller seemed to have been halted permanently. But it was not so. Russia has always shown great powers of recovery in war-time, and this was to be no exception. The greatest of the Russian efforts was yet to be made.

It came in June 1916. The Czar had re-equipped his troops and found a great commander, Alex Brusilov. Brusilov's armies faced the Austrians in the southern part of the long eastern front. Having noticed how the enemy had always been able to tell when a great attack was coming, Brusilov concealed his preparations with care. He then struck with great weight.

After three days the Austrian front before him almost dissolved into thin air. The roads were filled in every direction with the fleeing remnants of the Austrian armies. Day after day the world watched amazed as the armies of Russia, whom almost everyone had thought beaten, dealt a series of smashing blows. City after city which had been lost the previous year was recaptured. Bands of hard-riding Cossacks roamed and swept the countryside, harassing the retreating foe, penetrating the screen of infantry again and again, to capture guns and transport of all types. Desperate efforts were made to halt the advance, German soldiers being rushed in by rail from north, south and even across the whole width of Europe from France. They were brushed aside by the elated Russians: at first easily, then with rather heavier fighting as the advance moved on more steadily, and the weeks passed. Prisoners were taken in thousands, and the final total was probably about 400,000. The steamroller was rumbling forward at last!

It was four months before the advance was finally checked. On Brusilov's part of the front about one-third of the land lost the previous year after the Gorlice breakthrough had been regained. A terrible blow had been struck at the Austrian forces. Over many of the towns of Galicia the awful tide of war had flowed for the third time.

TURMOIL AND REVOLT: THE END OF CZARDOM

War imposes a tremendous strain on any nation, whether victorious or defeated. Coming after so much previous effort, and after so many months of weary conflict, the Brusilov offensive hit the hotch-potch empire of Austria-Hungary so hard that it never fully recovered. But Russia too was affected, far more than seemed obvious. Her victory had been gained at a great cost—too great, as it turned out. The drain of human lives, the shortage of food which was acute in Russia, and above all the prospect of the slaughter and the misery going on and on, led to a situation where the country was ripe for revolution.

Petrograd, the Russian capital (now called Leningrad), was the scene. There was rioting in the streets. Workers armed themselves and were joined by soldiers. Fighting broke out with the police. The fleet joined in the revolt. For a few days there was turmoil, but then all seemed to be over as a new Government was formed and the Czar resigned and was placed under arrest. All over the country workers, soldiers, farmers and others banded themselves into councils or 'soviets'. A spirit of excitement ran through the air, and there was a genuine feeling of brotherhood and the start of a new Russia which should be better than the old. This was in March 1917.

The new Government carried on the war for a little longer, making the great Brusilov commander-in-chief. In France and Britain there was great relief, for though there had been a time of doubt and indecision, it seemed that Russia was going to remain a member of the Entente.

The relief was rudely shattered in the autumn. The Germans had sent back to Russia an exile living in Switzerland called Lenin. He passed through Germany in a special sealed train, having no contact with the world outside. Once in Russia he aimed at a more far-reaching revolution which should make the country a completely Communist state. Together with others, he seized power in November 1917. From then onwards his only wish was to end the war with the Central Powers. But the Germans forced a hard bargain on them in the treaty which was signed at Brest-Litovsk in March 1918. It left Russia helpless from a military point of view, giving the Germans enormous tracts of land between the Baltic and the Black Sea; but more important still, it meant that the full weight of the German army, as well as Austrian and Turkish forces previously fighting Russia, could now be turned against the Western Allies. Over sixty German divisions, transported by the excellent German railway system, were transferred to the west. The French, British and Americans waited apprehensively for the blow they knew must soon fall.

The triumph of the Communists in Russia put the ex-Czar in a dangerous position. In July 1918 he and his family were imprisoned in a house at Ekaterinberg. An order arrived from Moscow, where the Communists had transferred the capital, and the whole royal family, with their servants and their dog, were shot. The long line of Russian emperors and empresses was ended, and a new age had begun.

8 In the Air

Zeppelins and Balloons

German Zeppelin *L.31*, flying near the battleship *Ostfriesland*

The German navy had placed great faith in the use of airships for 'spotting' purposes: they were the eyes of the fleet, and could range far out over the North Sea to tell of the position of Allied vessels by wireless. They were very valuable from this point of view. The British, on the other hand, lagged behind in naval airships at the beginning of the conflict, only gradually making up the leeway. Their Royal Naval Air Service had to make do at first with its few seaplanes. Meanwhile, the German airships kept their watch on the North Sea, spotted and reported submarines and warships, and even came down to intercept merchant ships on the surface.

Count Zeppelin had given Germany her great lead in the design of rigid airships, mainly in the twenty years before 1914. His huge craft, as well as the two other types of airship used by the Germans, flew higher than most planes, and for the first few months of the war there seemed to be little real defence against them. It was only a matter of time before they were used on bombing raids against British towns.

One day in January 1915, three Zeppelins left their bases and headed across the North Sea. Their cruising speed was less than fifty miles an hour, but they could if necessary stay aloft throughout the night and the whole of the next day. Bad weather interfered with their plans as they crossed the English coast, but seeing the lights of two sizeable towns below them they dropped bombs, killing a few unfortunate people at Yarmouth and King's Lynn. The British people had to face a new and unpleasant fact: the Royal Navy and the sea were no longer the complete protection they had been in previous centuries, for their enemy was now striking at them from the air.

The raids continued on suitable nights. The damage was not great, particularly if we think of the massed air attacks of 1940 and after. But war work stopped in many a factory as the air-

Zeppelin raid damage at Camberwell, London. Ten people were killed. It was the costliest raid of all to the Germans, for of the eleven Zeppelins which took off five were destroyed by the Allies or wrecked by a violent storm which came upon them over Britain and swept them helplessly southwards. October 1917

ships throbbed their way overhead, and planes were diverted from France for air defence work. As they became available, anti-aircraft guns and searchlight batteries were placed near the obvious targets. The defences of London were built up for the onslaught which would surely follow.

When they came, the London attacks did curiously little damage, though bombs hit various parts of the capital. Large numbers of people watched the searchlights and the shell-bursts during the raids, and on the night of 2 September 1916 they saw an awesome sight. *S.L.11*, picked up by the search-lights, was attacked by an aeroplane, and was soon a blazing mass tumbling earthwards from 12,000 feet. The crew were scorched to death, and today lie in the cemetery at Potters Bar. Within a month *L.31* and *L.32* had met the same fate. The night raiders were being mastered.

A NIGHT OF TERROR, 31 JANUARY 1916

Nell Bibby had been with her friend Doris to a new Girls' Club which had opened that night in the High Street, Burton-on-Trent. The two girls were talking excitedly as they walked home, at about nine o'clock. Both fifteen years old, they hoped very much that they would be allowed to attend the club again the following week.

A sudden bright flash lit up the buildings around, followed instantly by the sharp bang of an explosion. Others came after. The two girls, at first only half understanding that the city was being bombed, hurried on towards home. They passed down Station Street, and at the junction came upon a curious sight. The area was lit by some brilliant street lamps, and a crowd of soldiers clad in hospital blue had gathered and were trying to put them out. Some were even flinging their boots up at the lights. The girls hurried on, past the goods yard. There were other explosions, and the streets were full of hurrying soldiers. From somewhere near came the ringing of a fire engine bell. They were glad to reach Doris's home safely. It was hours later before they went to bed, and even then it was not to sleep.

The following morning revealed the extent of the damage. Rows of houses had been destroyed in several places. The goods yard had suffered a direct hit on some of the buildings there. Several bombs had hit brewery premises. Christchurch Vicarage and Mission Hall had been hit, and with terrible effect, for a meeting had been in progress at the hall and the bomb had killed the speaker and some of the audience. At Shobnall Street an eighteen-year-old girl had been killed, but one woman had had what seemed a miraculous escape. Upstairs in the house when it was destroyed, she had been holding a baby in her arms at the very moment the bomb exploded. Both her arms were broken, but the baby was safe, and she had no other serious injuries.

The girls had been fortunate, for heavy damage had occurred close to the route they had followed. The visit to the new club turned out to be the last as well as the first, for it did not open again.

Nine Zeppelins had made the raid. Merseyside had also been bombed. Three Zeppelins had attacked Burton, attracted by the glow of shop and street lights. For another airship, *L.19*, it was the last raid, for she had engine trouble and came down in the sea. There she drifted for at least two days, being seen by a trawler which refused to take off her crew. After that, she was never seen again, and undoubtedly lies somewhere beneath the North Sea.

Many other towns, particularly in the Midlands and on the east coast, suffered in the same way as Burton-on-Trent. London was the best of all targets, but the defences grew formidable. The raids tailed off towards the end of the war, when the heavy bombers took over. However, in 1918 the latest Zeppelins were wonderful machines. They were powered by six engines, each of over two hundred horse-power, and were held aloft in the air by more than two million cubic feet of hydrogen gas. Each was as long as eleven cricket pitches: nearly seven hundred feet.

Airships and aircraft were among the weapons used by the Royal Navy to defeat the U-boat offensive. By ranging out over the seas they forced enemy submarines to submerge, thus making it difficult for them to approach or overtake the convoys. At the same time the escorting warships could be warned of the presence of a U-boat.

A convoy is escorted by a British naval airship

Ships in convoy were also protected by the use of captive balloons. These were towed along by vessels specially adapted for the purpose. The observers telephoned their reports from their swaying baskets, dangling precariously beneath the gas-bag. Large man-carrying kites were used for the same purpose by the French, both on land and at sea, but their greater dependence on the wind made their value more doubtful and their use often dangerous.

Large numbers of balloons were used by the armies for artillery observation work. From his high position the balloon's observer would scan with his binoculars the area due to be shelled. He would watch carefully where the shells fell. If the range were incorrect or the direction wrong, this was tele-phoned to the ground and the next shots could be corrected. As soon as the target was 'registered' the order 'Gunfire!' would be given, and the objective would soon be covered with the smoke of bursting shells. Sometimes the registration was simply noted and the actual bombardment carried out later: perhaps to precede an infantry attack.

A *Caquot Kite Balloon* in the Somme area. The observer is clearly visible in his basket. Notice also the motor-winch, the communication-trench and the large number of horses tethered nearby

War Flying on the Western Front

Young Tom Aldous learned to fly—at his own expense—on the outbreak of war; he then joined the Royal Flying Corps. He flew the famous *F.E.2b*s, two-seater biplanes with open cockpits, the pilot sitting over the petrol tank and having only a simple windscreen for protection. The propeller was behind him, pushing the plane along in the midst of its kitelike framework of bamboo and cord.

Tom was a member of No 22 Squadron. They flew from a grass airfield near Amiens, carrying either bombs or a camera for photographing the German lines and communications.

'On my first patrol we were attacked by two Huns. We shot one down in flames and the other just pushed off. On our way home we saw an observation balloon. We dived on this balloon and brought that down in flames.' Most pilots and observers were not as fortunate as this, and airmen newly posted out from England were especially vulnerable until they had gained experience of war flying. Many lost their lives shortly after joining their squadrons in France.

One day a photograph showed something of unusual interest: the Germans were putting up a very large building some way behind their lines. It could be a Zeppelin shed. A bombing raid was ordered.

On the first perfect afternoon that came along Tom found himself flying his *F.E.* towards the area where the photograph had been taken. With him were seventeen other *F.E.2bs*; all flying at 10,000 feet. Five thousand feet below he could see other machines—eighteen De Havilland day bombers. High above, glinting in the sunshine was a formation of scouts, fast, single-seat fighters, ready to dive on any enemy plane which might try to attack the bombers.

The French landscape rolled steadily below as they pressed ahead. Then came the battlefield area, with the trench-lines zig-zagging their twisted way south towards Switzerland. They were over enemy territory. Puffs of black smoke began to appear among the machines as the German anti-aircraft guns —'Archie'—came into action. Some of the bursts were unpleasantly close, for this was 1917 and the ineffective anti-aircraft guns of 1914 had given way to heavier and better equipment on both sides.

With a sudden, sharp 'crack!' the *F.E.* shuddered. The engine had been hit. 'We've caught a packet,' yelled Tom to his observer. He turned the *F.E.* away from the formation and began the glide back in the direction of the lines. They were well inside hostile country: could they glide that far? Would they be intercepted on the way? If so, their chances of escape would be almost nil.

Some minutes later Tom brought the *F.E.* gliding over the German lines, having lost most of his height. There was the expected rattle of machine-guns as they passed over, and then Tom was looking for somewhere to make an emergency landing. He picked a field which seemed perfect. He could not see the telegraph wires which ran across it. They spelt disaster as the *F.E.* piled into them, and Tom soon found himself in hospital. Happily, his injuries were not serious.

It was found that the German shell which had brought the *F.E.* down had completely sheered off one of the cylinders of the engine. The other aircraft went on to destroy their target.

During the four years of war each side strove to outdo the other in the quality and quantity of its aeroplanes. Improvement was rapid as new designs followed one another. Engines

The famous *Sopwith Camel*, a fighter with a reputation for extreme sensitivity to the controls. This one is having its compass checked and adjusted. Notice the machine-gun

became more powerful and more reliable. Machine-guns, already dominating the trench warfare, became the supreme weapons of the air, replacing the pistols and rifles of 1914. Pusher aircraft, like the *F.E.2b*, gradually gave way to the 'tractors', with the whirling airscrew in front of the fuselage instead of behind it. Planes flew enormously increased distances, so much so that London was attacked by German *Gotha* bombers, and the British had begun by November 1918 to build up a powerful force designed to attack Berlin, a round trip of something like a thousand miles. The single-engined, kitelike planes of 1914, slow, ungainly and often unreliable, had been replaced by fast, smart scouts, like the *S.E.5* and the *Spad*, or the *Sopwith Camel*; whilst some bomber squadrons were being equipped with machines powered by two, three or four engines. The aeroplane had grown up during the war years.

The two sides honoured their successful pilots, especially the leading 'aces' of air fighting. The French had Navarre, with his crimson *Nieuport Scout*, scoring victories in the skies above Verdun, and the equally famous Fonck, who once destroyed six German planes in one amazing day. The Germans made heroes of Immelmann, Boelcke and the great Manfred von Richthofen, whose 'circus' of red-painted *Fokker* triplanes dominated for a time the Flanders skies. They were all fine pilots. Richthofen's toll of victories made him the idol of the

A German Twin-Motor Heavy Bomber, an *A.E.G. G(iv)*, shot down in Allied Territory, June 1918

German public, and his study walls were decorated with dozens of trophies cut from machines he had shot down. Like most of the other aces, he was eventually unlucky and was himself destroyed, putting all Germany into mourning. This was in April 1918. His funeral, behind the British lines, was an occasion for as much ceremony and as many wreaths from British squadrons as if he had been a popular R.F.C. officer, instead of one of their most dangerous foes.

The British too had their aces. The most famous of these was Albert Ball, a shy Nottingham lad who preferred to work alone, often stalking his opponent from beneath. At the age of twenty he brought sudden death to enemy after enemy during 1916, while the Somme battles raged below. He met the same end himself in the spring of 1917, during an encounter with the Richthofen circus.

Later in the war there were to be pilots like McCudden, Mannock and 'Billy' Bishop, the Canadian ace, who were credited with the destruction of even more enemy planes than Ball—a total of seventy-two in the case of Bishop. There were more aircraft in the skies as time went on, and the Allies were to finish the war with perhaps 8,000 aircraft in service all over the world. The Germans found themselves greatly outnumbered, having about 2,800. However, they certainly made good use of these.

The Royal Air Force was born during the war, when the

A *Friedrichshafen Seaplane* brings despatches to a German submarine in the Mediterranean. Calm weather was necessary for a safe landing on the water

'Billy' Bishop, the Canadian ace pilot, standing by his *Nieuport Scout* in August 1917. He was awarded the Military Cross, the Distinguished Service Order and the Victoria Cross, and was presented with all three together by King George V at Buckingham Palace. He was still serving in the Royal Canadian Air Force during the Second World War

Royal Flying Corps and the Royal Naval Air Service were united to form it. This was on 1 April 1918. Ten weeks later, one of the most significant air raids of the war took place, but it was one which showed that planes were to be of great importance to the world's navies. Seven *Camels*, each fitted out with two fifty-pound bombs, took off from a floating aerodrome: H.M.S. *Furious*, a converted battle cruiser. They attacked the German Zeppelin sheds at Tondern, and *L.54* and *L.60* went up in huge, billowing waves of flame. The day of the aircraft carrier had arrived. At sea as well as on the land, air power had become all-important. For attack and defence, photography and reconnaissance, both armies and navies needed the aeroplane.

The Apartment of Baron Manfred von Richthofen. It is decorated with relics of the machines he destroyed. To the Germans he was 'The Red Knight of the Air'.

9 The British People at War

A Changed Britain

When a Tommy got a 'blighty' (wounded so badly that he had to be sent back to England) he was often amazed at the changes which the War had brought about at home. It seemed to him that the whole way of life known to him before he went to France had disappeared. He would be very impressed by the advance in the status of women. This would perhaps be the first thing he would notice, because they would be scurrying about the railway platforms as porters and ticket collectors. If it were late in the War he would observe the early closing of the food shops . . . closing because they had sold out their stocks. There would be the prosperous workmen who had been required for essential industries and had therefore not joined up . . . prosperous because, unlike himself, they were paid a high wage and lived in comfort, a long way from the Western Front. He would not like many of the changes that he saw, for in some he could see a threat to his job and security when the war finished. These great changes were the result of a more prolonged struggle than had been expected in 1914. It began as a struggle between opposing armies on the battlefields. But it developed quickly into an exhausting struggle between desperate nations. Each country strove frantically to keep its armies supplied and active.

The 'Home Front' had come to be as important as the Front under fire.

Going to War

Despite the fact that volunteers poured into the recruiting offices in the first months of war, the ghastly slaughter made necessary the introduction of compulsory military service. It came in 1916, the year of the Somme, first for single men and later for married men. Conscription was new to this country. There were some people who objected to it on the grounds of religious beliefs. Special tribunals were set up to deal with these conscientious objectors. Under the stress of the war, how-ever, they were not treated very sympathetically; many were sent to prison (where fellow prisoners often maltreated them), and those who had their appeals dismissed were often posted deliberately to areas under heavy fire. Indeed it was alleged afterwards that some of these conscientious objectors were tied to posts known to be under enemy fire.

Women do their Share

The departure of so many men to the battle-grounds left a serious shortage of labour. Into the gap stepped women. On 18 July 1915, there was a great Women's War Pageant when

Girl munition workers stacking bullets at Woolwich Arsenal

thousands of women demonstrators marched for miles along the streets of London and sent a deputation to meet the then Minister for Munitions, Lloyd George. To him they pledged their assistance in the struggle.

This was really the beginning of an incredible change in the

Inside a shell-filling factory. The girls found that working with cordite gave them yellow complexions.

position of women. Before the war it had been considered beneath the dignity of a lady to have to work for a living. Indeed every obstacle had been put in the way. The woman's place was held to be very much in the home, subject to the husband of the house, shielded from the rough world of men, and with the smelling salts ever close to ward off the fainting fit. The Suffragettes had chained themselves to lamp-posts and smashed shop windows in an effort to shake off this Victorian picture of themselves and to obtain the right to vote.

With the war they were able to demonstrate practically their claim for equality with men. They took jobs as tram conduc-

A W.R.N.S. instructor teaches the use of gasmasks

tors, railway porters, chimney sweeps, coal merchants, and postwomen. They set up a Land Army and enrolled volunteers to work on the farms. Some joined the army, where they were employed in work away from the front. Nurses were often to be found with the doctors not far from the trenches. The casualty-clearing stations were full of women who before the war would rarely have ventured to do hard work.

Valuable and dangerous was the work done by the female munition workers. They filled the shells and packed the bullets. They worked long hours: twelve hours daily was quite common. They risked being killed in factory explosions. They contracted diseases from the T.N.T. they worked with, diseases which could turn their skins yellow.

The 'lilac and sun-bonnet brigade', as they were called, had earned their rights.

No more was the role of the woman to be despised. After their sacrifices in the great conflict, as a tribute to their work, the right to vote was given to women over thirty. Soon all women over twenty-one earned this privilege.

Food

'During January and February 1918 as many as one million people were standing weekly in the London area alone, waiting hour after hour for food which was often enough all gone before their turn came. On 21 January *The Times* reported: "The queues at the Smithfield around those butchers who do a retail trade were very large. At 11 o'clock one queue consisted of 4,000 people." And on 25 January: "Food queues were more numerous yesterday than they have been on any day this year. There were butter and margarine queues, meat queues, and—a new development—fish queues."'

We can see from the above accounts that the food shortage was beginning to make itself felt by the last year of the war. At first there were fairly good stocks and apart from rising prices the situation in the first eighteen months was stable. But since most of our food is imported the increase in sinkings which followed the U-boat campaigns began to have an effect. The situation was particularly critical early in 1917 when the U-boats were sinking our ships faster than we could replace them.

93

The steep rise in prices combined with the shortages meant that poorer people began to have difficulty where richer people did not. It also meant that some traders began to cash in on the scarcities and make money by selling only for the highest prices. The Government took action to ensure fair distribution throughout the community. Sugar was rationed, quickly followed by meat, butter and other fats. Meals in hotels were limited to certain times and specified amounts. A new loaf was introduced which contained potato flour mixed with the wheat: this was called 'standard bread' and its colour was nearer to grey than white. Sugar and chocolate coverings of pastries were forbidden. No expensive sweets were allowed. The amount of beer brewed was drastically reduced and the quality became poor. Before the end of the War, jam, marmalade and tea joined the ranks of rationed goods.

Despite these obvious hardships, however, it should be remembered that the Englishman at home fared better than his counterpart in Belgium, France, Poland or Germany. The Europeans not only went short of food but suffered the destruction of their homes and villages. The Zeppelins and the coastal bombardments did nothing like the damage that the engagements in Belgium and France did. (Even today farmers can still damage their ploughs on the buried debris.) The starving Berliners would gladly have changed places with the queueing Londoners in 1918. Bread, sugar and jam had long been a scarcity. Even the fuel to cook with was rare in 1918. When the British and American soldiers were billeted on Germans after the Armistice they found themselves sharing their own rations with their conquered hosts.

A Group of French schoolchildren wearing their gasmasks. The school was at Rheims. This is a good example of the way the war affected absolutely everybody in the European countries taking part.

10   Animals in the War

A True Incident

Len Russell raised himself cautiously from his hiding place. The plane had gone, but pandemonium reigned in the camp. Horses were screaming and rearing. Officers shouted orders. He glanced towards the tent. It was in shreds, but the men seemed all right. He turned his attention to the frightened horses.

It was a pitiful sight. Some twenty lay on the ground, killed outright by flying bomb splinters. The rest were hysterical. His own horse, Dolly, spotted him as he picked his way across the dead bodies. She lurched towards him, shaking her head vigorously.

'Whoa girl, whoa there!' he said, trying to calm her. She had been struck in the forehead and was bleeding profusely. Desperately she tried to shake off the protruding splinters. Len patted her on the neck and wiped the blood from her face. She screamed and stamped her hoof. Sadly he made his way with her towards the veterinary surgeon's tent.

There were dozens of horses waiting at the tent, stamping, snorting and whinneying. He tried to close his ears to the sound of the officer's pistol, busy behind the tent.

A few moments later the surgeon glanced over the wounds. He shook his head and waved Len and Dolly to the rear. There was nothing that could be done. For Dolly this was the end of the road. For Len it meant parting with the faithful friend of the last two years.

The sharp crack of the gun rang in his ears for long afterwards.

Horses like Dolly played a notable part in the war. Although motor vehicles were coming into use in thousands, the transport on both sides was still largely horse-drawn. Apart from

A shell finds a mark. A limber has been caught by shellfire, and two of the horses killed. The photo was taken during the German spring offensive, 1918

pulling wagon-loads of supplies and provisions all but the largest guns depended on teams of horses for their mobility. The cavalry regiments too, though mostly held in reserve, were still expected to play an important part in exploiting the long-awaited breakthrough, when it should come. So many horses were needed by the army that in the early days of the war it was necessary to stop horse-drawn vehicles in the streets of English towns and commandeer them, despite the strong protests of the owners.

The animals, too, faced the horrors of war: death by gassing, bombing and gunfire.

Near the front line in France, where in many places the going became very bad, wheels sank into the mud, so that the carts and limbers had to be replaced by pack-mules.

It was usual to take supplies up to the line under cover of darkness. Often the enemy would have the supply route pinpointed, and would drop in the occasional shell during the night in hope of hitting the lines of wagons which he knew would be on the move. Bridges and cross-roads were favourite targets, and the limber drivers would hurry past these thank-fully.

One of Len Russell's first experiences of battle also concerned a horse. He was seventeen at the time, and had been made 'lead of the gun'—in charge of the horses which pulled one of the howitzers of his battery. It was night-time, and the sergeant's own horse, Dixie, was in his care to hold as well as the gun horses. All was quiet. Orders had been given: no smoking, no talking. The signal for action was awaited.

With startling suddenness a star-shell burst overhead, lighting up all around. In terror, Dixie reared on her hind legs and then bolted. Amid the confusion she was quickly lost in the darkness, and Len never saw her again, though he searched all the following day. He remembered that night more vividly for the sergeant's curses than for the shells which exploded nearby!

A German star-shell lights up the darkness. A remarkable night photograph taken at Ploegsteert, near Ypres. The troops called it Plugstreet

97

Another incident was more humorous. Gasmasks were issued. These consisted of hoods, drawn right over the head and tucked into the neck of the tunic. It was important that the horses grow accustomed to seeing their drivers in these monstrosities:

'We lined up behind the horses. The sergeant barked out the orders, and the masks were hastily donned. We were told to step forward. The horses took one look at us in the masks and shied, kicked, reared and bucked in their stalls. It took a long time before they realized who we were.'

Horses too needed gasmasks. Orders emphasized that these were to be fitted before putting on one's own mask. As you can imagine they were awkward, cumbersome affairs, and the horses did not like them at all.

When, in the winter, battlefields and forward areas wallowed in mud, the horses often had no alternative but to stand in it, sometimes for hours at a stretch. In the very cold weather they could be trapped as the mud froze solid. Occasionally transport became so bad that fodder and water could not be brought up for days on end, and the animals would be on short rations. But the work of supplying the guns had to go on.

'The order would arrive to take ammunition to the gunners, but the horses were so weak that they could hardly stand. I remember some of them just lying down and "giving their necks". They simply wanted to die. When they did this we had to pour water in their ears to make them stand up. It was an unwelcome and heartrending task.'

The problems of using animals in these conditions increased greatly later in the war when mules very often had to be used instead of horses. Mules, as you know, are inclined to be very stubborn at times. There was one occasion when Len had volunteered to carry rations to the howitzer crew, one and a half miles away. On paper this does not seem a difficult task, but to get to the crew meant ploughing through mud knee-deep for much of the way, with the whole area under fire from enemy artillery.

Len loaded up the animal and set off on the dangerous mission. At first things went smoothly, the mule ignoring the shells overhead. But as soon as the area of mud was reached she stopped in her tracks and refused to take any further steps at all. Len pushed and pulled; he tried every trick he knew to make the animal move, but in vain. It seemed she had absolutely made up her mind not to get her feet wet. Just imagine Len's feelings in this situation! In the end he was forced to leave the mule and wade through the mud on foot, with the valuable supplies on his own back. And when he returned, hours later, there she was, contentedly waiting for him by the side of a derelict tank! For completing his mission successfully Len was mentioned in official despatches.

Besides horses and mules, the Great Powers made use of dogs during the war. The Russians of course used thousands of sledge dogs in the bitter winters of the Eastern Front. The French trained and used dogs for carrying supplies and equipment of all sorts.

Dogs were often employed on dangerous work. This one was a carrier employed by the French. He is seen with his load of grenades

French Red Cross dogs were used to seek out wounded men on the battlefield, and many lives were saved by them. They were most valuable at night, when human eyes were at a disadvantage. The French thought so highly of their war dogs that they were once honoured by a special gathering in Paris, attended by the war leaders as well as many of the animals with their masters.

British and German dogs were used chiefly for message carrying. In the early days of the conflict British motor-cycle scouts sometimes took with them messenger dogs which had been locally trained. These were usually carried in a rickety sidecar, and could be sent back to base with a written note attached to the collar when there was anything to report.

99

The animals were well cared for, and if ill or wounded there were special 'dog hospitals' behind the front, like the one shown in the illustration.

Dogs proved faithful servants to both sides. Here is a German dog hospital behind the lines. Wounded dogs are being treated

In Belgium, where the people were accustomed to seeing light 'dog carts' in the streets, the larger breeds were even harnessed to pull machine-guns. They worked in pairs, and the gun would be mounted between two wheels very like those used on a bicycle.

The breeds utilized for all these purposes varied greatly. Huskies and wolfhounds, sheepdogs, alsatians and labradors all played their parts, but so did others, many mongrels among them. And for the Red Cross work the smallest breeds did just as well as their larger cousins.

Messages were not only carried by dogs. Pigeons were pressed into service in very large numbers, and the armies ran their lofts behind the lines. Thousands of reports and requests were carried to and fro by the birds, and some of them were of vital importance. You will be glad to know that the pigeons suffered very few casualties, unlike the horses and mules.

Carrier pigeons were useful when neither wireless nor telephone was available. Here a motor-cyclist sets off for the line with four pigeons

One French pigeon was made a member of the Legion of Honour for its flight through a storm of fire at the battle of Verdun in 1916. It carried important despatches. A British bird gained equal fame for bringing S.O.S. messages on several occasions from sea plane crews forced down in the North Sea. Each time, the men were saved.

One unit which caught the public imagination was the Imperial Camel Corps, which was stationed in the Middle East. In difficult desert regions the camels proved cheaper and more reliable than the motor cars of those times. But perhaps even more interesting is a report about the goods which were being shipped through the Arctic to the Russian port of Archangel. After unloading, the cargoes had to be taken south:

'For the transport of ammunition and light articles a large number of reindeer were available, and the endless stream of reindeer sleighs winding over the snowy plains of Lapland was one of the most picturesque episodes of the war.'*

Even this does not exhaust the list of animals pressed into use by the struggling nations of Europe. Ox-teams drew heavy guns, donkeys toiled through narrow Alpine passes in never-ending lines, and the Germans even took from the Hamburg Zoo an elephant which had been a favourite with the children there. Her name was 'Jenny', and she was sent to northern France to do her bit for the Fatherland. Her great strength enabled her to do the work of a powerful tractor.

With animals being used in such large numbers the veterinary corps of the various armies were of vital importance. They did excellent work, and tried to make the lives of the creatures under their care as pleasant as possible. Conditions were frequently so bad that there was a constant procession of sick animals through the veterinary hospitals; and after artillery bombardments there was often a stream of injured horses to attend to.

* Sir Henry Newbolt, *History of the Great War, Naval Operations* (vol. V, p. 301)

Bullock carts being used to transport shells in Serbia, 1916

A German field hospital. An operation is being carried out on a horse

Sick horses on the way to a German veterinary hospital

11 Spies : The Secret Armies

An incident from the Eastern Front: Lieutenant Boleslavski was a cavalry officer with the Russian army.

Lieutenant Boleslavski was disturbed. It was just one and a half hours since he had received his orders to take the village from the retreating Germans. His mission had been accomplished swiftly. Within an hour the huge anti-aircraft guns were secretly and silently assembled in the nearby woods. Now, half an hour later, those same guns were in ruins. Heavy German fire had wreaked havoc among them. How had they known that they were there? How had they known the correct time to fire?

He ordered a thorough search to be made of the village. All inhabitants were under suspicion. All the surrounding fields were to be combed. No effort must be spared in tracking down the leak of information.

The source of the leak was quickly discovered. An insulated wire was found in a small creek. It was traced back to a nearby barn. Inside, the wire led straight to the carcass of a recently slaughtered calf. A telephone was concealed within the dead body!

The farmer and his wife were arrested. In their own house they were court-martialled, and under questioning admitted that they had sent the information to the Germans. There was only one sentence for spies: death. In the early light of the new day the farmer and his wife were hanged from the same branch of a nearby tree.

In all probability the farmer and his wife were forced by the retreating Germans to agree to send information. Terrified of the consequences of refusing they had agreed . . . to their cost. For to be proved a spy in wartime meant the ultimate penalty with little delay.

The spies of the armies were their secret eyes. On the information transmitted to headquarters by the secret agents much military strategy might depend. Information about the movement of troops, especially large movements, about the whereabouts of ammunition dumps, or of specially arranged train loads, all might be the clue to a new enemy offensive.

The farmer and his wife were unwilling amateurs. But even the professional might have been found in their role at some time during his career. The spy had to go into the enemy camp. He had to be trusted by the enemy. He must not arouse suspicion by being too inquisitive. All his actions should seem natural. If he were caught there would be no one to rescue him. He fought alone. Obviously spies were people of considerable talents.

The war produced many outstanding spies on all sides. Charles Lucieto was a notorious French spy. Not only did he manage to visit Germany and obtain information of value to the Allies, but he claimed to have entered the German Legation in Berne and defied all the booby traps left for the unwary intruder. After the war he described the room of the German Minister to Switzerland in detail, mentioning trapdoors under the carpet, electrified keyholes, and hidden bells under some of the floorboards.

Miklos Soltesz, otherwise known as Nicholas Snowden, was an Austrian spy and was just eighteen when the War broke out. During his time he gave service on both the Russian and Italian fronts. One incident which he recalled began in a railway carriage en route to the Italian front. He became suspicious of a girl who was sleeping in the corner and who in her sleep began murmuring about the Austrians being 'bandits'. He noticed that her brooch appeared to be rather larger than would be expected on a lady and very gently he removed it from the sleeping suspect. On investigation a fine piece of paper was found to be concealed in the brooch.

At that moment the girl started and jumped up. Realizing that she was discovered she flung herself through the nearest doorway despite the fact that the train was moving. Soltesz pulled the communication cord and the train ground to a creaking halt. A search was made along the embankment, but without success. While engaged in this search a train approached from the opposite direction, and before the startled Soltesz and his companions could do anything, the girl appeared, and flung herself aboard the last swinging carriage, to disappear into the darkness.

On investigation it was found that the small piece of paper contained a plan of all the Austrian defences along the Adriatic coastline. Such information would have been of immense value to the Italians.

As this story indicates, there was plenty of scope for women in spying. Less suspicion was likely to fall on an innocent-looking girl following her business. Marthe McKenna was a famous Belgian spy. She was a nurse and spent her time treating the German wounded. She was often able to pick up information while going about her normal duties. Sometimes she found herself in the position of betraying the lives of the very same soldiers whom she had nursed back to health in the hospital. When the Germans finally detected her they were amazed that one who had shown such devotion to her nursing duties and worked so hard to attend to the German wounded could actually go so far as to betray them. Marthe did not expect any mercy, but she was one of the few spies whose life was spared. In recognition of her nursing services to the German soldiers Marthe McKenna was reprieved and sentenced to imprisonment.

Many other spies were to achieve fame—or death—for their exploits behind enemy lines. In view of their activities it was not surprising that occasionally 'spy mania' broke out and the general public began to attribute any unusual sights and sounds to 'spies'. Suspicious noises would be investigated . . . just in case. Innocent people might be questioned for hours because they had perhaps left a light showing at night or made an unusual journey. Box numbers in newspapers were traced and checked: the secret armies worked through all channels!

12 Different Viewpoints

On pages 108 and 109 you will find two newspaper reports. One is British, the other from a well-known German newspaper, the *Frankfürter Zeitung*. Both deal with the same events: the first day's fighting in the Somme offensive, 1 July 1916.

A translation of the German report appears on page 110.

Read the two extracts and you will see immediately that they are written from widely different viewpoints. The British account stresses the good points and ignores the bad, such as the extremely heavy casualties of the day's fighting. The German account does the same, making out that the Allied gains are quite negligible, and that the German soldiers retreated not because they were forced to, but because 'it was preferred'. Who would have realized from the British report that this was the most disastrous day in the whole history of the British army? What German, reading his newspaper, could have guessed that German Headquarters was disturbed and shaken by the great power and violence of the Allied assaults?

This is a good example of the way nations are prepared to delude themselves during wartime. It is almost always the enemy who suffers the heavy losses, very rarely oneself. Unpleasant facts are not faced or are treated as being less serious than they really are; points which make pleasant reading are given a prominent place. Often even official reports distorted the truth . . . on both sides, Allied and enemy.

Think of the war at sea. To the Germans the Royal Navy's blockade was a wicked, inhuman attack upon the innocent civilians of Germany, causing illness and misery among women, children and even babies. On the other hand, U-boat successes were hailed with delight, and jubilant postcards commemorated the end of the *Lusitania*. Needless to say, the British held exactly opposite opinions, and to many the U-boat men were simply murderous pirates.

'To Paris!' shouted the eager German soldiers in August 1914. 'To Berlin!' cried their French opposite numbers. How

GREAT OFFENSIVE CO

British Capture Fricourt and Make Prog East of Village and Near La Boissell

FRENCH PIERCE FOE SECOND LINE

Our Ally Also Takes Two Villages, Strong Ge Positions. Guns and Captives.

"THE GENERAL SITUATION IS FAVOURABLE

(BRITISH OFFICIAL.)

GENERAL HEADQUARTERS, Sunday, 10.15

Heavy fighting has taken place to-day in the area between the and the Somme, especially about Fricourt and La Boisselle.

Fricourt, which was captured by our troops about 2 p.m., remain hands, and some progress has been made East of the village.

In the neighbourhood of La Boisselle the enemy is offering a st resistance, but our troops are making satisfactory progress.

A considerable quantity of war material has fallen into our but details are not at present available.

On the other side of the valley, on the Ancre, the situa unchanged.

The general situation may be regarded as favourable.

Later information of the enemy's losses show that our first es were too low.

Yesterday our aeroplanes were very active in co-operation w attack north of the Somme, and afforded valuable assistance operations.

Numerous enemy headquarters and railway centres were at with bombs.

In one of these raids our escorting aeroplanes were attack twenty Fokkers, which were driven off.   Two enemy machine seen to crash to the earth and were destroyed.

Some long-distance reconnaissances were carried out in s numerous attempts by enemy machines to frustrate the enterpris

Three of our aeroplanes are missing.   Our kite balloons were air the whole day.

BRITISH CAPTURE 3,500 PRISONERS.

General Headquarters, Sunday, 5.5

Substantial progress has been made in the vicinity of Fricourt, was captured by our troops by 2 p.m. to-day.

Up to noon to-day some 800 more prisoners have been taken operations between the Ancre and the Somme, bringing the total 3,500, including those captured on other parts of the front last nig

"ALL DAY FIGHTING IN OUR FAVOUR."

(FRENCH OFFICIAL.)

PARIS, Sunday.— The following official communiqué was issu

JES—9,500 PRISONERS

Map showing Thiaumont Work.

DIVISIONS THAT HAD TO BE WITHDRAWN.

ns Admit Front Line Was Penetrated.

LLIES HEAVY LOSSES."

(GERMAN OFFICIAL.)

ERDAM, Sunday.—To-day's German communiqué says:—

ern Theatre of War.—Yesterday a nglo
l d
reso
ive
a n
n on
re,
aind

MIGHTIEST BATTLE OF BRITISH ARMY.

Eye-Witness's Thrilling Story of Start of Great Bombardment.

TERRIFIC DRAMA.

"The Present Offensive Has a Definite Object."

BRITISH HEADQUARTERS, FRANCE, Saturday.—The secret has been well kept. The weeks of essential preparation and concentration have passed without attracting the least degree of suspicion that anything beyond the normal was in progress, so unobtrusively and even stealthily has the immense task been carried out.

Down to quite lately I had heard officers seriously discussing the improbability of an

---

E

ISH
Ger
ixte
ssell
rint
t to
oner

CH
quin
Fri

IAN
tria

IAN
ialic
oner

Jomm
e, b
oth
fore
us to
uent
fro
ches
ositi
sual
idly
was
ane
re w

Der englisch-französische Angriff

Schwere Verluste der Gegner ohne nennenswerte Vorteile.

15 feindliche Flugzeuge abgeschossen.

Fortschritte an der Ostfront.

Großes Hauptquartier, 2. Juli. (W. B. Amtlich.)

Westlicher Kriegsschauplatz.

In einer Breite von etwa vierzig Km. begann gestern der seit vielen Monaten mit unbeschränkten Mitteln vorbereitete große englisch-französische Massenangriff nach siebentägiger stärkster Artillerie- und Gasvorwirkung. Auf beiden Ufern der Somme, sowie dem Ancre-Bach von Gommecourt bis in Gegend von La Boisselle errang der Feind keine nennenswerten Vorteile, erlitt aber sehr schwere Verluste. Dagegen gelang es ihm, in die vordersten Linien der beiden an die Somme stoßenden Divisionsabschnitte an einzelnen Stellen einzudringen, so daß vorgezogen wurde, diese Divisionen aus den völlig zerschossenen vordersten Gräben in die zwischen erster und zweiter Stellung liegende Riegelstellung zurückzunehmen. Das in der vordersten Linie freineshaute

wrong they all were! The sadly unbalanced, ill-informed out-
looks of the European peoples helped to prolong the war for
four ghastly years.

Translated from the *Frankfürter Zeitung.*

ANGLO–FRENCH OFFENSIVE

ENEMY'S HEAVY LOSSES AND NEGLIGIBLE GAINS

15 Enemy Planes Shot Down

. . . . . .

Advance on Eastern Front

. . . . . .

General Headquarters, 2 July
Correspondent: W. B. Amtlich

Western Theatre of War

After a whole week of the most heavy artillery and gas
bombardment, there began yesterday on a broad front of about
forty kilometres the great Anglo–French massed offensive,
which has been under preparation—with limitless resources—
for many months.

On both banks of the Somme, from the river Ancre at
Gommecourt to the La Boisselle area the enemy gained no
advantage worth mentioning, but suffered heavy losses.
Nevertheless, on both French and British Somme fronts their
assault troops managed to penetrate our front line in isolated
spots. It was preferred therefore to withdraw our divisions
from the front-line trenches, which had been completely
destroyed by heavy fire, to the reserve line between the first
and second positions.

As is usual in such circumstances, some material—permanent fixtures of the front line—having been rendered use-
less, was lost.

13 The Land War III

The year 1917 saw the war becoming more grim, more bitter, and more apparently hopeless than ever. The British Regular Army had disappeared long before in the fruitless battles of 1914 and 1915. The Kitchener Armies had suffered terribly in the Somme battles. But still the build-up of British strength continued, assisted by the compulsory military service adopted in 1916. Guns, ammunition and stores of all kinds had become plentiful as the Entente nations marshalled all their energies for war production. The numbers of planes and tanks available had increased and would continue to grow. The resources of both the British and the French Empires were being used with good effect against Germany: Australian and Canadian troops in particular were to play a large part in the last two years of war. In addition, a small number of United States soldiers arrived in France in June, and they were the forerunners of a great host to follow.

For the French, 1917 saw high hopes of success. Their new commander had gained some startling successes in the Verdun area, and thought he could repeat this on a much larger scale. His attacks in Champagne broke down with huge loss of life, since the enemy had known in advance what was coming. Mutiny broke out in the French Army, and a grave situation arose. General Pétain did his best to restore morale; some mutineers were executed by shooting or shellfire. Had the German command known the situation they could well have advanced against an enemy quite unprepared to meet them. But they disbelieved the reports that came to them, and the units affected were gradually won back to their duties.

Vital High Ground: Vimy Ridge and Messines Hill

In the north, the British prepared a series of attacks near Arras. One of the most remarkable features of these was the part played by the Canadian Corps, which helped to capture the vital, strongly fortified Vimy Ridge. Some idea of the

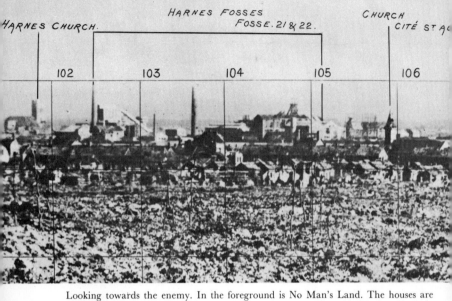

HARNES CHURCH.   HARNES FOSSES   CHURCH   FOSSE. 21 & 22.   CITÉ ST A

102   103   104   105   106

Looking towards the enemy. In the foreground is No Man's Land. The houses are those of the French village of Cité St. Auguste, near Lens. The complicated German trench system ran round and through the village, parts of it passing between the

immense organization necessary to mount the attack may be gained from the Canadian Army's Official Historian:

'Within the Canadian forward area more than twenty-five miles of trunk road had to be repaired and maintained; the construction of new routes included three miles of plank road. A system of twenty miles of tramway in the Corps area was reconditioned and extended. Over these rails light trains drawn by gasoline engines, or more often by mules, hauled forward daily 800 tons or more of ammunition, rations and engineer stores: and there were some 300 push trucks for evacuating wounded. The sudden concentration of 50,000 horses within a restricted area where very little water existed necessitated the large-scale construction of reservoirs, pumping installations and forty-five miles of pipe lines in order to meet the daily requirements of 600,000 gallons. In order to ensure good communications in the Canadian zone, signallers added to existing circuits twenty-one miles of cable, burying it seven feet deep to withstand enemy shelling, and sixty-six miles of unburied wire. As the area was in full view of the enemy, most of this work had to be done at night.'

CHIMNEYS
FOSSE. 2. & 2. BIS.   DUMP OF
                    P.25   FOSSE. 7. & 7. BIS.
CH.   0. 23. A &
FOSSE. 9 & 17.   HOUSES.
        0. 14. A & B.   N. II. A. 35. 85
LOUETTE   DUMP   FOSSE. 7. & 7. BIS.
    HAROLD CORONS   P. 25.   CITE. ST. PIERRE   MONTIGNY C.

108   109   110   111   112

houses and the camera. There were two further trench systems beyond the village.
October 1917

Sappers dug deep tunnels leading up to the front lines. Twenty-five feet or more below ground, they provided safe cover for troops to move and for the establishment of storage depots and first aid posts.

The attack came in April, and was brilliantly successful. The whole of the important high ground was wrested from its German defenders, and their commander, Prince Rupprecht, ordered a withdrawal to a third defence line, about four miles to the east. Vimy was later selected as the site for a memorial to the 50,000 Canadian soldiers who died in France.

Two months later there was another successful attack, this time at Messines, near the old battleground of Ypres. Over a distance of eight miles the guns were massed: one every twenty yards or so. The immense barrage lasted more than a fortnight and was rounded off by the detonation of nineteen huge charges of explosive, placed beneath the German positions by mining engineers. Messines Hill erupted with smoke and flame, and the thunderous noise rolled all over Northern France. The defenders were demoralized, and the hill captured.

113

The village of Wytschaete, ruined by bombardment. It was captured by Irish troops after the attack on Messines Hill, June 1917

Passchendaele: Battle in the Mud

Haig, the British commander, made the greatest effort of the year during August, September and October. He wished to thrust through the enemy near Ypres, and free some of the Belgian coastline from German occupation. You will remember that Belgian harbours were being used by the U-boats, which at this time were still threatening the destruction of British commerce. The battle is often called 'The Third Battle of Ypres'—the first two having been in 1914 and 1915 (see pp. 12 and 20).

The weather was atrociously bad. The flat plain which was the fighting area became a pock-marked swamp, every shell-hole filling with water. Mud made life all but impossible. Yet the slow struggle forward went on. Instead of freeing the Belgian coast the offensive merely brought a few shattered villages under British control, and at an appalling cost in lives: the casualties totalled a quarter of a million. German figures admit the loss of 217,000 men. Both armies suffered badly in morale, and the name of Passchendaele has become notorious. Many years afterwards, Len Russell still preserved

The Menin road near Ypres, familiar to countless thousands of British soldiers, many, many of whom lie today in the huge cemeteries nearby

a vivid recollection of the clinging slime and the mud-filled shell-holes into which the war had turned a fertile countryside of rich farmland (see p. 98).

(see p. 98)

A German pill-box in the Ypres salient. It had been captured by Australian troops, October 1917

Tanks

In England fertile and inventive minds had been at work on the problem of the Western Front. An answer to the massed rifles, machine-guns and barbed wire of the trenches had at last been found. This was the tank, a heavily armoured vehicle mounted on caterpillar-tracks. The development of these armoured monsters was partly due to the interest shown in them by Mr Winston Churchill, at the Admiralty.

Two prototype tanks were demonstrated secretly in February 1916. They were called 'Big Willie' and 'Little Willie' (after the Kaiser and his son!), and although they could only travel at 2 m.p.h. they did cross obstacles successfully and were a 'hit'. Mr Balfour, a Cabinet Minister present, went for a ride in one and when he experienced difficulty in clambering out was eventually hauled out feet first!

Major-General Swinton of the Royal Engineers was given the task of supervising the building of a further 100 tanks. This was done in the greatest secrecy and to disguise their purpose they were described as 'water tanks' (their appearance resembled this). He advised that they be used in great numbers and that they should not be launched on unsuitable terrain.

Unfortunately Major-General Swinton's advice was not carried out immediately. In view of great losses in the Somme fighting Sir Douglas Haig decided to use the first of the newly completed machines as they reached the front line in September 1916 (see p. 27). The result was that the secret was given away with little success in return. Some tanks foundered in the deep mud and others wandered off course. Where a tank was successful it was not supported by numbers and, therefore, there was no follow-up.

However, at least the tanks had had a trial experience. Fortunately the Germans did not attach much importance to the new machines, and at Cambrai in November 1917 they proved their real value.

Major-General Swinton's advice was this time adhered to. Some 350 tanks assembled under cover of darkness and mist along a front six miles long. In the pale light of the early dawn shortly after 6 a.m., the rumbling metal monsters rolled forward to the accompaniment of an artillery barrage. The tangled masses of barbed wire shivered and crumpled before the grinding tracks. The first line of German trenches fell quickly, the troops scattering and fumbling before the advancing mass of mobile armour. . . . The portable bridges carried on top of the tanks enabled further ditches to be crossed. In all an advance of six miles was achieved in twelve hours, impressive figures when one remembers similar advances taking three months before tanks were used.

The tank went on to be used in ever-increasing numbers. It proved one of the greatest factors in the ending of the deadlock of trench warfare.

A Mark 2 tank, ditched in crossing a communication trench captured from the Germans, near the town of Arras, 1917

Ludendorff's Great Last Gamble for Victory

1918 . . . and the Germans, despite their brilliant victories in the east, faced a desperate situation which promised to grow worse with every month that passed. The odds were mounting against them.

1 The Allied blockade was restricting industry and sapping the strength of the people. 1917 had been a terrible, hungry winter

for the ordinary folk of Germany. Another winter at war would mean starvation and ruin.

2 American strength was growing. If the war went on her enormous manpower would produce large armies of young and enthusiastic troops.

3 The British and French efforts were already gigantic. Their industries were pouring out munitions in such quantities that they could equip not only their own men but the new American armies as well. The British Empire had become an enormous arsenal of men and materials.

4 The U-boat campaign had failed (though only just) to bring the British to defeat.

There was one bright spot. Using troops transferred from the east the Germans might manage to overwhelm the British and French before the superiority of numbers passed from them for ever. Ludendorff prepared his armies for a series of tremendous blows. The British were to be the main target.

Storm-troops were specially trained for the massive assaults. Colonel Brüchmüller, the artillery expert, concentrated his

At the German Headquarters. Hindenburg is on the left and Ludendorff on the right, with the Kaiser between them

thousands of guns and howitzers for the mightiest effort of his career.

21 March 1918 saw the Spring Offensives open. Germany's future was staked on their success. Allied troops were smothered by a storm of gas shell, blasted and hammered by high explosive and shrapnel. Trenches and dugouts were obliterated, barbed wire torn aside and telephone lines fractured. The British Fifth Army bore the brunt of the assault, and its forward troops were decimated by the gunfire. The stormtroopers burst through the few remaining positions under a blanket of heavy mist, the defenders unable to see anything till they were overwhelmed. The Germans swept on, passing by pockets of resistance, hurling their stick-bombs as soon as they met the dazed defenders.

Ten days later the attack petered out. But a breakthrough of forty miles had been achieved in places, much of this over the old nightmare battleground of the Somme. Ludendorff turned elsewhere.

The March attack was repeated in the next four months

March 1918: the German bombardment destroys a British 18-pounder battery

Battlefield scene on 23 March 1918. A Mark 4 tank in Peronne, just behind the front where the German attack fell

against both British and French, in Flanders and on the front nearest Paris. Each time the storm-troops broke through, but even as they reached the open country beyond the trench lines they found the resistance stiffer and stiffer as reinforcements were brought in, and new defences were dug and wired. They captured great amounts of food, ammunition and stores, but these were easily replaced from British stocks within days. At one time the world waited breathlessly as Paris seemed threatened again as in 1914, and a second battle of the Marne was fought to save the city; again the Germans were beaten back, this time with American soldiers joining the counter-attacks. The fury of the German attacks was tremendous, but although they could break through the trench and battle zones, they could not break through the Allied armies which retreated before them, gathering reinforcements as they went.

The pace and strength of the Spring Offensives forced the Allies to appoint a single commander for all their armies. Differences between the British and French were forgotten in face of the great common danger, and Marshal Foch took supreme control.

The Allies Hit Back

The German attacks petered out in failure, and the time was ripe for the Allies to hit back. 8 August was the day—'the black day of the German army', as Ludendorff later called it. Australian and Canadian soldiers led the attack, backed up by six hundred light and heavy tanks. Mist helped the attackers, as on 21 March. Again, there was a breakthrough, but this time in the opposite direction.

The whole front flared up as the British and French commanders ordered new attacks. As the resistance stiffened, so the attack would be transferred elsewhere. The German retreat was steady but definite. Fighting hard, they were pushed back to their rear positions, or to new fortifications hastily prepared. The American army attacked near Verdun, clearing the Germans from an extensive 'salient' which jutted out into the French line. Then came a smashing blow in the north: the German Siegfried defence line was breached, and British and Americans poured through the gap. All along the line, the Germans were on the retreat: still under control, still fighting, but nevertheless withdrawing from the

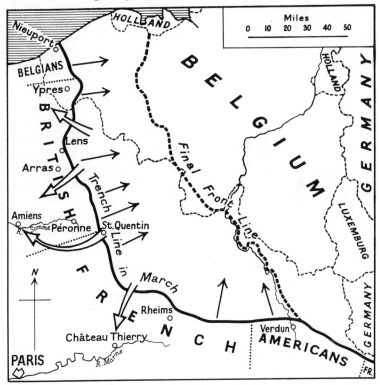

Ludendorff's Last Gamble; and the Allied Advance. Hollow arrows show the Spring offensives; single arrows the Allied advance after 8 August 1918

Armies have to be kept supplied. This demands careful organization on a vast scale. Here limbers are being unloaded to form a roadside shell-dump at Drocourt, in October 1918

countryside they had held for four years. From Verdun to the North Sea, the Allied armies were at last on the advance.

Defeat

THE GERMANS FALL BACK

Alvin York's marksmanship. An episode in the retreat.

'On 8 October, a patrol of twenty men under a sergeant were probing forward to find and eliminate some machine-gun posts holding up the general advance, when they came to a dell containing some seventy-five German troops. Either through immediate shock of surprise or recent disintegration of morale, the Germans promptly surrendered, but the Americans were now observed by the machine-gunners they had been sent to find: these swung their guns around and with their customary efficiency, shot down the members of the patrol until there were only eight Americans left.

'Fortunately, one of these was a Corporal York, a large man from Tennessee, who had passed his formative years shooting for the pot in countryside not dissimilar to that in which he now found himself. From a kneeling position he shot the machine-gunners—all of them—and when a German infantry lieutenant led a charge of half a platoon along the edge of the dell towards him, York continued to pick them off one by one until his rifle ammunition was gone, whereupon he

A German machine-gunner lies beside his gun, September 1918

drew his ·45 automatic and continued a deliberate and accurate fire until the survivors of the charge threw down their arms and joined their compatriots already lying flat in order to avoid the stray bullets.

'Action now ceased and York marched his prisoners back towards the American lines where, after an unavoidable misunderstanding over identity, he handed them over to a lieutenant who asked how many there were.

'"Heck, Lieutenant," said York in one of those classic replies of military legend. "I ain't had time to count them yet!"'

Misgivings in Berlin

The massive Spring Offensive had failed. Throughout August the news trickled in of German reverses. They were now losing the places which they had held since the outbreak of the War four years previously. The German High Command quarrelled among themselves as to the action to be taken. Their allies began to crumble: in September Bulgaria and Turkey suffered heavy defeats. In defiance of the German pleas Austria-Hungary declared her intention of making peace.

Ludendorff wavered uncertainly. He found difficulty in formulating a plan. Finally, in October, he decided that the best that the Germans might hope for would be to consolidate on a shortened front on the German frontier itself. An armistice would very conveniently give their troops the necessary time to withdraw behind the border. There it would be relatively easy to supply the forces who would perhaps fight more ferociously in defence of their own native soil.

Realizing that the British and the French would probably see straight through this plan it was felt that the approach for such an armistice would meet with a kinder reception from President Wilson. Accordingly contact was made with him on 4 October. But the folly of German leadership once again revealed itself. On 10 October two passenger ships were torpedoed off the coast of Ireland with reported losses totalling 800 lives. Bodies were washed up on the coast for weeks afterwards, constantly inflaming opinion against the Germans.

President Wilson was infuriated. He had already replied to the first German Note in mild terms. His Note of 14 October was very different: he could not possibly consider an armistice while the German forces continued 'illegal and inhuman practices . . . acts of inhumanity, spoliation, and desolation, which the Allied nations justly look upon with horror and with burning hearts'. He stated that for armistice conditions the Germans would have to deal with the Allied military commanders who would be entitled to demand security for their own military supremacy. He even hinted that a change of leadership in Germany might be necessary before an armistice. It was the confidence of imminent victory that inspired this rousing condemnation of the German Government.

In an act of bravado this Note was rejected. But the German Government reckoned without their own people. The population was war-weary and starving. Thousands were dying of a new menace, Spanish influenza, mainly because their resistance to disease was weakened as a result of prolonged starvation. Riots and revolutions began to break out in the major cities. Deserters from the front swelled the angry mobs. The sailors on board the ships in the port of Kiel mutinied and soon some 40,000 armed men were on the move, setting up local councils similar to those which had appeared in Russia during the Revolution. The Red Flag flew over many German buildings.

The news came of the Turkish armistice of 30 October, followed by the Austrian on 3 November. The German Government tottered. Ludendorff was dismissed. But the abdication of the Kaiser was now the demand of the population. The end was in sight. In the face of the opposition surrender was accepted. Representatives sought out Marshal Foch and offered unconditional surrender.

'What do you want, gentlemen?' asked Foch.

'Your proposals for an armistice,' they replied.

'Oh, we're not making any proposals for an armistice,' said Foch. 'We are quite happy to go on fighting.'

'But we must have terms,' they protested. 'We cannot continue the conflict.'

'Ah! You come to ask for an armistice? That is a different thing.'

Here is a summary of the main terms of the Armistice which Foch handed to the German delegates:

Immediate evacuation of all occupied territory.

Evacuation of the west bank of the Rhine by all forms of German military force (also places on the east bank).

Repatriation of all Allied prisoners of war and of all civilians.

Surrender in good condition of the following:

5,000 heavy and field guns.
25,000 machine-guns.
3,000 trench-mortars.
1,700 aeroplanes.
All German submarines.
6 battle-cruisers.
10 battleships.
8 light cruisers.
50 destroyers.

The Germans were to pay for the damage incurred as a result of the war (reparations).

Cancellation of Brest-Litovsk treaty with Russia.

The German delegates were aghast. They dare not agree to such demands. They asked for time to consult their Government and it was granted. Pending the acceptance of these terms it was agreed that the ceasefire would begin on Monday, 11 November, at 11 a.m.

They returned to Berlin where they found a new Government: the Kaiser had abdicated and fled to Holland. The new Government accepted the Armistice proposals. The Great War was ending in defeat for Germany.

The Ceasefire

The clock ticked slowly and time passed. Morning on 11 November dawned mistily at first, but soon it became fine. The soldiers stared out towards the enemy's lines with mixed feelings. They had their orders: 'Stand fast on the line reached at 11 a.m.' Until then 'they' were still the enemy, to be despised, repulsed and annihilated if possible.

At some points it was decided to sit out the remaining few hours and merely to watch for a sudden attempt to obtain a last-minute gain. At others fighting was continuous right up until the last moment. There was an attempt by the British at 10.50 a.m. to take a bridge over a river by sending in a cavalry charge. They were mown down by the German

Two commanders meet. Sir Douglas Haig in conversation with Marshal Foch, just after the Armistice

machine-guns and the position was only taken when the Germans laid down their arms on the stroke of 11 a.m. in accordance with the Armistice terms.

In places there were still occasional bursts from artillery after the appointed hour, but gradually the firing died down. Stillness settled over the shell-torn landscape.

The soldiers could hardly believe that peace was really with them. For some time many remained in their hiding-places, avoiding exposing themselves in a manner which four years of warring had taught them. Here and there the adventurous emerged and stood upright, surveying the land for the foe of the previous hour. A few groups got together and exchanged conversations and cigarettes. But soon orders forbade such fraternization. The ceasefire did not necessarily mean peace to the politicians. After the struggle in the field the struggle in the conference room was to come.

The Ceasefire in London

The strokes of 11 o'clock were greeted very differently at home. Everyone appeared to rush out into the streets to celebrate. There was dancing, singing, cheering and yelling. Vehicles and buses were crowded: the whole population it seemed had stopped work. Sir Winston Churchill described the scene:

'It was a few minutes before the eleventh hour of the eleventh day of the eleventh month. I stood at the window of my room looking up Northumberland Avenue towards Trafalgar Square, waiting for Big Ben to tell that the War was over. . . . My mind mechanically persisted in exploring the problem of demobilization. What was to happen to our three million munition workers? What would they make now? How would the roaring factories be converted? How in fact are swords beaten into ploughshares? How long would it take to bring the armies home? What would they do when they got home? . . .

'And then suddenly the first stroke of the chime. I looked again at the broad street beneath me. It was deserted. From the portals of one of the large hotels . . . darted the slight figure of a girl clerk. . . . Then from all sides men and women came scurrying into the street. Streams of people poured out of all the buildings. The bells of London began to clash. Northumberland Avenue was now crowded with people in hundreds, nay, thousands, rushing hither and thither in a frantic manner, shouting and screaming with joy. I could see that Trafalgar Square was already swarming. Around me in our very headquarters . . . disorder had broken out. Doors banged. Feet clattered down corridors. Everyone rose from the desk and cast aside pen and paper. All bounds were broken. The tumult grew. . . . Flags appeared as if by magic. . . . Almost before the last stroke of the clock had died away, the strict, war-straitened, regulated streets of London had become a triumphant pandemonium.'

The Great War was over! This was the cry. All the suffering seemed momentarily forgotten in the first flush of victory.

14　Making the Peace

The Treaty of Versailles

In January 1919 the victorious powers met for the peace conferences. In reality there were a series of treaties signed:

Treaty of Versailles with Germany.
Treaty of Saint-Germain with Austria.
Treaty of Neuilly with Bulgaria.
Treaty of Trianon with Hungary.
Treaty of Lausanne with Turkey.

The principles on which the various treaties rested were known as President Wilson's Fourteen Points, which he had published before the War ended. Here they are:

1　No more secret diplomacy (referring to the secret alliances which had existed before 1914).

2　Freedom of navigation at sea. (America had disapproved of the way in which the British Navy had stopped and searched ships that were suspected of trading with Germany during the War.) Lloyd George stated that Britain would not accept this point.

3　Regulations which prevented international trade should be swept away.

4　National armaments were to be reduced.

5　Claims to colonies to be settled by considering the interests of the colonies themselves. . . . (Germany lost all her colonies.)

6　Russia to be free to develop her own system of government.

7　Belgium was to be evacuated and restored.

8　Alsace and Lorraine were to be restored to France. (Germany had seized these in 1871.)

9　The Italian frontiers should be revised to take into account the wishes of the people.

10　Peoples of the Austro-Hungarian Empire should be given their freedom.

11　The Balkan peoples to be free to form their own nations.

12　Peoples in the Turkish empire to be allowed the same; the Dardanelles to be kept open to all ships.

13　Poland to be re-created with access to the sea.

14　A general association of nations to be formed to look after the interests of all: The League of Nations.

Europe in 1914

What the Treaty actually did : Summary

A. GERMANY

Lost Alsace and Lorraine to France.

Lost Malmédy and Eupen to Belgium.

Lost parts of East and West Prussia to Poland.

Lost some coalfields in Silesia to Poland.

Her navy was limited to six light battleships.

Her army was limited to 100,000, with no conscription.

The building of warships, aircraft, and tanks was forbidden.

No troops were allowed in the Rhineland.

Was forced to accept full responsibility for the War and had to agree to pay reparation. Thus France was given the Saar coalfields by way of compensation.

All German colonies lost.

Europe after the Versailles Treaty, 1920

Comment. The Germans were not allowed to discuss these terms but were merely handed them to sign.

The reparations clause proved very difficult to enforce: after all, although it seemed obvious to everyone that Germany ought to pay for the damage she had done she was in no state to pay anything in view of the effect of the war itself. In the end the problem was left to an International Commission which was to meet from time to time and set the amount.

B. OTHER ARRANGEMENTS

The Empire of Austria-Hungary was broken up: Austria was reduced to a very tiny state, as was Hungary. A new state was created on the southern frontiers of Austria and Hungary called Yugoslavia. This included Serbia, Bosnia and

131

Herzegovina. In the north, Czechoslovakia and Poland were
created.

New republics of Finland, Latvia, Lithuania and Estonia
were created. Rumania was enlarged. Italy got parts of the
Austrian Tyrol and Trentino area.

The Scuttling of the Dreadnoughts. The *Derfflinger* slips beneath the waves, Scapa
Flow, June 1919. The great battleships of the High Seas Fleet, together with many
other German vessels, were surrendered to Britain by the Armistice terms. Their
skeleton crews sank them rather than hand them over to the Royal Navy. German
submarines surrendered at Harwich

The League of Nations

The League of Nations was created to provide opportunities
for governments to co-operate together and thus to avoid
struggles like the Great War. In 1918 much was expected of
the League in ending the possibilities of further wars. But the
League soon got into difficulties. For one thing the Germans
were not allowed to join at first and therefore they always
tended to look upon it as a 'club' for the victorious Powers.

Then the Americans withdrew from it, going back to their pre-war policy of 'Isolation'. And later still the Great Powers found themselves unwilling to use their joint force in order to preserve the peace. It was a brave attempt to avoid future wars, but the old suspicions were too deeply rooted for it to succeed.

Germany Signs the Peace Treaty: A Bitter Moment

Scene: The Hall of Mirrors in the Palace of Versailles
Date: 28 June 1919.

'The delegates arrive in little bunches and push up the central aisle slowly. Wilson and Lloyd George are among the last. They take their seats at the central table. The table is at last full. Clemenceau glances to right and left. People sit down . . . but continue chattering. Clemenceau makes a sign to the ushers. They say "Ssh! Ssh! Ssh" . . . People cease chattering and there is only the sound of occasional coughing and the dry rustle of programmes. The officials . . . move up the aisle and say "Ssh! Ssh!" again. Then there is an absolute hush, followed by a sharp military order. The Republican Guards at the doorway flash their swords into their scabbards with a loud click. "Bring in the Germans", says Clemenceau. . . .

'Through the doors at the end . . . come four officers of France, Great Britain, America and Italy. And then, isolated and pitiable, come the two German delegates, Dr Müller, Dr Bell. The silence is terrifying. Their feet upon a strip of parquet . . . echo hollow and duplicate. They keep their eyes fixed away from those two thousand staring eyes, fixed upon the ceiling. They are deathly pale. They do not appear as representative of a brutal militarism. The one is pale and pink eye-lidded: the second fiddle in a Brunswick orchestra. The other is moon-faced and suffering: an ordinary private. It is almost painful. . . .

'There is general tension. They sign. There is general relaxation. Conversation hums again in an undertone. . . .

'Suddenly from outside comes the crash of guns thundering a salute. . . . Through the few open windows comes the sound of distant crowds cheering hoarsely. . . . There was a final hush. . . .

'We kept our seats while the Germans were conducted like prisoners from the dock, their eyes fixed upon some distant point of the horizon. . . .'

Counting the Cost

The nations took stock of their shattered world. Between them, on the battlefields, in the air and on the seas, or simply through starvation and disease, they had lost over ten million lives, perhaps many more than this if we think of those millions who simply disappeared in the chaos and turmoil as the conflict raged across their homelands in Russia, France, Serbia and a dozen other countries. Another twenty millions had been wounded.

But figures like this are difficult to understand. They come to life with terrible meaning only if we think of them as the countless husbands, brothers and sons who had marched off to the military depots and joined the troop trains, never to return; or as the numberless friends, fiancés, relatives and neighbours who in future must choke and wrestle for breath as the result of gassing, or who would live on through the years only as invalids. This, to multitudes of human beings just like ourselves, was the price of it all.

The nations had to pay in other ways too. Allied and enemy governments found themselves burdened with enormous debts, some of which have never been repaid to this day. Britain, in 1914 a creditor nation drawing huge sums from abroad by way of interest on loans, found in 1918 that this great income had dried up, for the investments had been sold to pay for war material. Worse still, the prosperity everyone hoped would return with the peace showed very little sign of reappearing. The utter exhaustion of the European states was to slow their recovery for years.

The War had been vaster in scope than anyone had thought possible in 1914. There had been wars fought all over the world before, but never before had the nations been locked in such a titanic, mortal struggle, with every factory, workshop, mine, dock and railway controlled and directed for the war effort by their desperate governments. Agriculture, industry and commerce had become the weapons wherewith the civilian armies had toiled and sweated for the victory. How were they to be put on a peacetime footing again?

In addition to these problems, which they shared with everyone else, the Germans smarted under the feeling that the peace treaty had dealt with them harshly and spitefully. Dissatisfaction and resentment prepared the way for a man like Adolf Hitler. The First World War was to have a sequel in 1939.

Things to Do

to Madras and Pondicherry, to Diego Garcia, to the Cocos Islands. (Your total will be an underestimate.)

9 Find out the differences between a battleship and a battle-cruiser of the 1914 period.

Chapter 4

10 Use a modern atlas to find out in which country Tannen-berg and the Masurian Lakes are today.

11 Use a geography book or an encyclopaedia to discover what conditions are like in winter in the areas covered by the Eastern Front.

Chapter 5

12 What are the widths of the Dardanelles (*a*) at their narrowest, (*b*) at their widest? How far is it from Mudros to Constantinople?

How do you imagine that a submarine commander would navigate through the Straits?

Chapter 6

13 Write a paragraph from the German point of view on the sinking of the *Lusitania*. Take account of the fact that the Germans had warned travellers against sailing on the ship by means of an advertisement in a New York newspaper.

14 In the library look up the following personalities of Jut-land, making brief notes on each:

Admiral Scheer; Admiral Jellicoe; Admiral Beatty.

15 For discussion: Was the British Government justified in not telling the nation how near it was to defeat in April 1917?

Chapter 7

16 Draw and label a sketch map showing the German empire in Africa in 1914.

17 Write three short paragraphs on Caporetto as follows:

(*a*) from the point of view of an Italian soldier;
(*b*) from the point of view of an Austrian soldier;
(*c*) from the point of view of a British observer.

18 Design a postage stamp commemorating the capture of Tsing Tau by Japan.

19 Using the library find out more about President Woodrow Wilson.

20 For discussion: Why did the United States remain neutral for almost three years of the conflict?

21 Look up in the library Lawrence of Arabia (T. E. Lawrence) and write ten lines on his exploits with the Arabs.

22 Compose a telegram such as might have been sent by the British ambassador in Petrograd, informing the British Government of the Russian Revolution in the spring of 1917.

23 Find out more about the life of Lenin and his importance.

Chapter 8

24 Compile a small folder of work on the development of the aeroplane during the First World War.

25 Draw a black and white sketch showing a night raid over London by Zeppelin.

Chapter 9

26 Find out more about the suffragette movement. When did all adult women finally obtain the vote?

Chapter 10

27 Design a poster praising the work of animals in the war.

Chapter 11

28 These three people all have something in common:
Mata Hari;   Roger Casement;   Edith Cavell.
Look them up and find out the link.

Chapter 12

29 Find examples from today's newspapers of subjects on which the nations of the world have very different viewpoints.

(If you study a foreign language try to obtain a newspaper in it to compare with British reporting.)

Chapter 13

30   Why do you think some French troops mutinied in 1917? Was the action taken against them justified?

31   It has been suggested that if Alvin York had tried his feat on the Germans in 1914 or even before the spring of 1918 the end of his story would have been very different. Why might this be so?

32   Find out the part played by Winston Churchill in the War.

Chapter 14

33   The Germans were very angry with the terms of the Treaty of Versailles. Which terms do you think they objected to most?

34   For discussion: Why did the treaty-makers impose harsh terms on Germany in 1918?

Would Germany have acted very differently had she been victorious? (The terms of the Brest-Litovsk Treaty will help this discussion.)

35   What was the special difficulty about 'making Germany pay'?

36   Draw a simple sketch map to show Austria-Hungary in 1914 and then draw a further map to show the same area after the War.

Can you find out roughly how long the Austro–Hungarian Empire had been in existence before 1919?

37   Write a few lines on what happened to Serbia after the War.

38   Write a paragraph on each of the following:

Clemenceau;   Admiral Roger Keyes;   Mustapha Kemal; Pétain;   H. H. Asquith;   J. C. Smuts;   Sir Douglas Haig; General Pershing;   E. Ludendorff;   P. Hindenburg;   Lloyd George;   Sir E. Allenby;   Marshal Foch.

Further Reading

Books Useful for Information about the War

CYRIL FALLS, *The First World War*. Longmans.

WINSTON CHURCHILL, *The Great War*. George Newnes.

R. R. SELLMAN, *The First World War*. Methuen.

A. J. P. TAYLOR, *An Illustrated History of The First World War*. Hamish Hamilton.

C. R. M. F. CRUTTWELL, *A History of the Great War*. O.U.P.

HANSON BALDWIN, *World War One*. Hutchinson.

A. H. BOOTH, *The True Book about the First World War*. Fred. Muller Ltd.

R. THOUMIN, *The First World War*. Secker & Warburg.

Some Interesting Books to Read

J. REMAK, *Sarajevo*. Weidenfeld & Nicolson.

BARRIE PITT, 1918 *The Last Act*. Cassell.

BARRIE PITT, *Zeebrugge*. Cassell.

ALAN MOOREHEAD, *Gallipoli*. Hamish Hamilton.

D. MACINTYRE, *The Wings of Neptune*. P. Davies.

K. MIDDLEMASS, *Command The Far Seas*. Hutchinson

K. POOLMAN, *Zeppelins Over England*. Evans Bros. Ltd.

A. A. HOEHLING & M. HOEHLING, *The Last Voyage of the Lusitania*. Longmans.

A. A. HOEHLING, *Edith Cavell*. Cassell.

Mr. Punch's History of the Great War. Cassell..

T. E. LAWRENCE, *Seven Pillars of Wisdom* (an abridged version). Penguin Modern Classics.

A. WHITEHOUSE, *The Years of the Sky Kings*. Macdonald & Co.

B. GARDNER (Editor), *Up The Line to Death*. Methuen.

Index

Index

Index

Year by Year: *The Major Events of the War*

YEAR	GENERAL	WESTERN FRONT
1914	Assassination of Archduke Ferdinand (June)	
	General war breaks out (August)	Schlieffen Plan
	Bombardment of Hartlepool, Scarborough, etc.	First battle of Marne
	Fall of Tsing Tau	First battle of Ypres
1915	Italy joins the war	Second Ypres
		Germans use poison gas
	Gallipoli	British and French breakthrough attempts
1916	Conscription in Britain	Verdun
	Lloyd George replaces Asquith as Prime Minister	Somme
1917	America joins war	Arras (Vimy Ridge)
	Italians driven back at Caporetto	
	Turks defeated	Third Ypres (Passchendaele)
		Cambrai (tanks)
1918	Royal Air Force formed	German Spring Offensive
	Armistice (November)	Second Marne
		Final Allied Offensive

EASTERN FRONT	AT SEA
Battles of Tannenberg and Masurian Lakes	*Goeben* and *Breslau* escape Heligoland Bight *Emden*'s exploits Coronel and Falklands
Breakthrough at Gorlice Russians driven back	*Lusitania* sunk
Brusilov's breakthrough	Jutland
Revolution in Russia	Greatest losses of ships to German U-boats
Russia out of war: Treaty of Brest-Litovsk	Zeebrugge